WILD ABOUT TURKEY

Tantalizing Tastes of Turkey and all the Trimmings,
With Recipes for Thanksgiving. . . and Beyond

NATIONAL
WILD TURKEY
FEDERATION

Cover and Book Designer: Kenner Patton
Front Cover Photography: courtesy of The National Wild Turkey
Federation and the National Turkey Federation
Back Cover Wild Turkey Photograph: Donald M. Jones
Camouflage Background: courtesy of Realtree Advantage
Recipe Editor: Ed Bamberger

Copyright © 1996
by The National Wild Turkey Federation

This book, or any portions thereof, may not be reproduced in any
form without written permission from the publisher, The Wimmer
Companies, Inc., Memphis, Tennessee.

Library of Congress Card Catalog Number: 95-61803
ISBN: 1-879958-30-9

For additional information about
The National Wild Turkey Federation, call
1-800-THE-NWTF.

To order additional cookbooks, use the order form
in the back of the book.

PREFACE

What is it about the National Wild Turkey Federation that makes us the fastest growing and one of the most successful conservation organizations in the nation? It's respect for the flag, regard for religion, and emphasis on family. These may not seem related to conservation, but they are. The NWTF is a "people organization," and it's my opinion that our members are the best people America has to offer. In my travels I constantly point out that people, not dollars, are what work for the wild turkey. Sure, people work to raise important funds, but it's the "people" part that makes things happen. Member and chapter contributions, fund-raising events, special projects, and the contributions of NWTF's corporate partners produce millions of dollars for conservation.

Thanks largely to dedicated professional state wildlife researchers and managers, the wild turkey is now the most widely distributed game bird in North America. Thanks to our equally dedicated NWTF members, the Federation has proved to be the most effective game bird conservation organization in the country.

Even though we passed the 120,000-member mark in our 22nd year, we must not rest on our laurels. It is easy for large organizations to get lured into perpetually growing their membership rolls for the sake of numbers, but the NWTF has always kept the wild turkey resource and the turkey-hunting tradition in sharp focus. That's the way it has to be. Our mission statement so dictates. Although we're proud of our accomplishments, we are making long-range plans to forge ahead with our multifaceted programs. It's the only way we can hope to preserve a hunting heritage for those who come after us.

In this excellent cookbook families and friends from across the country have brought their best "to the table" for your enjoyment. We invite you to join the NWTF team (application on page 251) and become a part of this great success story. Meanwhile, enjoy your wild turkey feasts.

Rob Keck

WILD ABOUT TURKEY

TABLE OF CONTENTS

INTRODUCTION

There was a time, and not so long ago, when we wouldn't have needed a wild turkey cookbook. In 1945, the wild turkey was barely hanging on in remote tracts. We had almost lost the only game bird that can bend a limb.

It's a familiar story to most NWTF members. When Europeans arrived, wild turkeys were present in abundance, and we know they ranged in areas that now touch at least 39 states and a small piece of southern Ontario, Canada. Thanks to the visionaries who finally started protecting remnant flocks, and to those who later figured out how to live-trap and move birds, today we have wild turkeys and turkey hunting seasons in 49 of the 50 states. Only Alaska has no wild turkeys.

In his 1994 book *Turkey Calls—An Enduring Folk Art*, Tennessee author Howard L. Harlan, in reference to turkey hunting, reminds us that "no other hunting sport has ever revisited its golden age." That is a remarkable fact, and we, as sportsmen and sportswomen, can't afford to forget it. Nor should we forget those who snatched the wild turkey from the brink of oblivion.

The most significant device used in wild turkey restoration was, and is, the cannon net, which was first used to capture wild turkeys in 1950, in South Carolina. The concept was sound. The design was appropriately modified, and the net's efficiency was quickly established. Its use soon spread to other states. The trap-and-transfer movement was under way.

In the 1960s came tiny radio transmitters that could be attached to wild turkeys to monitor their whereabouts. For the first time, wildlife scientists could locate and study this wary species in all seasons, which enabled them to document the bird's complete life history and apply that knowledge to its management.

The National Wild Turkey Federation was incorporated in 1973. The timing couldn't have been more right for a not-for-profit conservation group dedicated to conserving the wild turkey and preserving the wild turkey hunting heritage. The NWTF succeeded because we knew that if turkey hunters didn't unite and speak up for the wild turkey, nobody would.

Today resident wild turkeys occupy more square miles of habitat than any other resident game bird species in America, and the NWTF has members in all 50 states and several foreign countries and is still growing. Led by sportsmen and sportswomen and fed by a cadre of volunteers who raise most of its funds, the NWTF is committed to habitat improvement, hunter safety training, starting new flocks in all available habitat, and maintaining public awareness of the value of the wild turkey and other wildlife.

Through partnerships with industry, public utilities, government, colleges and universities, and private landowners, the NWTF is pledged to the task of helping carry wild turkey restoration and management into the next century. Assuring future hunting opportunities is certainly part of the plan, for there's no greater thrill in the outdoors than hearing a gobbling wild turkey and watching him strut into view.

We hope you and your family enjoy your wild harvest, and that you will help us impart to the next generation an appreciation for the outdoor life and for the bountiful blessings enjoyed today in America. Ours is a system of wildlife management unique in all the world. It produces abundant renewable wildlife resources and allows a controlled annual harvest. It works because ordinary people care about wildlife.

Enjoy these tasty dishes, and give thanks, with us, for the wild turkey and for those who guard its future.

Gene Smith

DEDICATION

This cookbook is dedicated to the thousands of National Wild Turkey Federation volunteers working across this great land for one of America's greatest wildlife resources, the American wild turkey.

Our volunteers are the lifeblood of the NWTF. The individual member. The turkey hunter. The conservationist. The sportsman who decided to put something back. The one who helped make the NWTF the acknowledged conservation leader it is today.

We dedicate this book to you not only for what you have already achieved for the resource but also for what you are now poised to accomplish in the future.

We honor you for the important part you play in raising funds, teaching hunting safety and ethics, encouraging young sportsmen and sportswomen, and providing improved wildlife habitat. We salute you for having led the way in your community and state to create a higher level of awareness and appreciation of the wild turkey. In short, we honor you for having put your money, your time, and your hard work squarely on the line for wildlife.

I know you'll agree that working for the wild turkey is a most rewarding and gratifying experience. Imagine what the world would be like if everyone moved forward with the positive, can-do attitude you exhibit.

Thank you, NWTF volunteer, for giving so freely to ensure the success of The National Wild Turkey Federation.

Carl Brown

Special thanks to all those members who contributed the delicious recipes to this cookbook effort, to Kenner Patton of Birmingham, Alabama, for his cover and cookbook design, and to artist Peter Ring for the portraits and sketches throughout the book.

BEFORE THE FEAST...OR ANY TIME

Appetizers to Snack, Beverages to Sip, Soups to Slurp, Breads to Sop

To me, the American wild turkey is the epitome of complete majesty, unmatched grace, total nobility, striking beauty, pure wildness, and unsurpassed cunning and wisdom. He is both my beloved friend and respected opponent of forest and field—the most worthy and challenging adversary I have ever had the privilege to duel. I hunt this magnificent and respected adversary with a clear conscience and with apology to no man. I pursue him not for that occasional and hard-won victory, but for the excitement of our duel in the remote swamps and lonesome mountainsides, for the thrill of seeing his great tracks etched in sand, glimpsing his black blur in golden oaks, then hearing the boom of his alarm putt and winged escape. These are the magic ingredients that stir the caveman corner of my soul and draw me like a sleepwalker from the clanging anthill city into his wild and remote lairs.

Dave Harbour, 1920-1988
Hunting the American Wild Turkey, 1975

TURKEY PÂTÉ

2 tablespoons unsalted butter
¼ yellow onion
1 teaspoon minced garlic
1 teaspoon ground thyme
1 (4-ounce) can mushrooms
1 pound turkey livers
2 tablespoons dry sherry
Freshly ground pepper to taste
Fresh parsley, chopped

Melt butter in large heavy skillet. Add onion, garlic, thyme, mushrooms, and livers, and sauté until livers are fully cooked, yet tender. Cool. Transfer mixture to food processor; add sherry and pepper. Cool. Mold into desired shape. Transfer to airtight container, cover, and chill at least 8 hours or overnight. Roll in parsley.
Serve with crackers or party-size rye or pumpernickel bread.
Yield: 6 or 8 servings

TURKEY TIDBITS WITH CRANBERRY DIP

½ **cup sour cream**
1 **tablespoon lemon juice**
1 **teaspoon prepared horseradish**
¼ **teaspoon salt**
1 **pound turkey breast tenderloins, cut into 1-inch pieces**
⅔ **cup breadcrumbs**
⅔ **cup ground walnuts**
2 **tablespoons butter, melted**

CRANBERRY DIP

1 **cup jellied cranberry sauce**
¼ **cup sour cream**
2 **teaspoons prepared horseradish**

In medium nonmetal bowl, blend sour cream and next 3 ingredients. Add turkey; toss to coat well. Cover; marinate in refrigerator 2 to 24 hours. Grease a 15x10x1-inch jellyroll pan. Combine breadcrumbs and walnuts in a bowl. Coat drained turkey pieces in breadcrumb mixture. Place turkey on pan. Drizzle with butter. Bake at 350° for 35 to 40 minutes, or until thoroughly cooked and golden. Make dip by blending cranberry sauce, sour cream, and horseradish. Serve turkey with dip.
Dip may be prepared 24 hours in advance.
Yield: 6 to 8 servings

Phyllis Cupit
Hermitage, TN

TURKEY RUMAKI

2 (1-pound) turkey breasts
¼ cup dark soy sauce, or enough to coat
½ teaspoon salt
1 teaspoon orange zest
1 to 2 teaspoons light sesame oil (optional)
8 ounces tawny port or dry vermouth
4 bacon strips, halved lengthwise and quartered
1 (8-ounce) can sliced water chestnuts, drained

Debone turkey. Cut meat into bite-size pieces, and place in medium bowl. Add enough soy sauce to cover meat, and the next four ingredients. Cover bowl and refrigerate for 1 hour. Wrap a bacon square around a water chestnut, then a turkey piece, and secure with a toothpick. Broil until bacon reaches desired doneness. Serve immediately.
Yield: 4 servings

Gary Dubay
Urbandale, IA

CHEESE BALL

1 (8-ounce) package cream cheese, softened
1 (8-ounce) tube hickory-smoked cheese, softened
1 (16-ounce) package processed cheese loaf, softened
1 teaspoon garlic powder
Chili powder, as needed

In a medium bowl, combine cheeses and garlic powder. Cover with wax paper and refrigerate for 1 hour. Form into 2 large or 3 medium balls and roll in chili powder. Soften 30 minutes at room temperature before serving.
Can be stored in refrigerator up to 2 weeks, or in freezer for up to 3 months.
Yield: 18 to 20 servings

Ivy Coffey
Russell, IA

TURKEY CHEESE BALL

1 (8-ounce) package cream cheese, softened
1 cup cubed cooked turkey
¾ cup slivered toasted almonds, finely chopped
⅓ cup mayonnaise
2 tablespoons chutney, chopped
1 to 3 teaspoons curry powder
¼ teaspoon salt
Chopped parsley, as needed

Combine cream cheese and next six ingredients. Shape into ball, and roll in parsley. Refrigerate for 3 to 4 hours. Let stand 30 minutes before serving.
Garnish with freshly cooked artichoke leaves. Serve with crackers.
Yield: 6 to 8 servings

Pat Spangler
Manchester, TN

NANCY'S CHEESE BALL

2 (8-ounce) packages cream cheese, softened
2 tablespoons minced onion
¼ cup crushed pineapple, drained
2 tablespoons finely chopped bell pepper
2 teaspoons seasoned salt
2 cups chopped pecans, divided

Combine cream cheese, next four ingredients, and 1 cup pecans until well blended. Form into ball and roll in remaining pecans. Chill at least 2 hours to combine flavors. Remove from refrigerator 30 minutes before serving.
Serve with crackers.
Yield: 8 to 10 servings

Nancy DeLoach
Saluda, SC

TURKEY SATAY

½ cup dark soy sauce
½ cup vegetable oil
1 cup brown sugar
½ cup chopped onion
½ lime, juiced
½ cup cilantro leaves, minced
1½ pounds turkey strips, cut into 5-inch strips
8 small bamboo skewers

THAI PEANUT SAUCE

1 cup coconut milk
2 tablespoons chunky-style peanut butter
1 tablespoon lemon juice
1 tablespoon dark soy sauce

Combine soy sauce and next 5 ingredients in medium bowl. Immerse bamboo skewers in water to cover, about 5 minutes. Skewer turkey strips and transfer to 11x7x1½-inch rectangular pan. Pour soy mixture over turkey strips, and toss to coat well. Cover and refrigerate for 2 hours. Grill over hot coals for one minute on each side or until tender. Prepare Thai Peanut Sauce by thoroughly combining all ingredients. Serve sauce as dip.
Yield: 6 to 8 servings

Masterbuilt Manufacturing, Inc.
Columbus, GA

DEEP-FRIED MUSHROOMS

1 pound fresh morel mushrooms
Salt
Flour
Vegetable oil

Slice mushrooms lengthwise and soak in saltwater for 4 hours. Drain mushrooms well. Dip each mushroom in salt, then in flour. Deep fry until lightly golden, being careful not to overcook. Drain on paper towels. Serve immediately.
Best when cooked same day as mushrooms are picked.
Yield: 4 to 6 servings

Rebecca Nix
Mount Vernon, IL

CHEESE WAFERS

1½ cups sifted flour
½ teaspoon salt
⅛ teaspoon red pepper
1 stick chilled butter, cut into bits
1 (8-ounce) package sharp Cheddar cheese, coarsely grated
40 whole pecans (optional)

Mix flour, salt, and red pepper in a medium bowl. Cut in butter with a pastry blender and combine until mixture resembles coarse meal. Add cheese and toss to mix. Form into log, wrap in wax paper, and refrigerate at least 8 hours or overnight. Carefully remove wax paper. Cut log into ¼-inch-thick slices. Top each slice with a pecan, if desired. Lightly grease cookie sheet. Bake at 375° for 10 to 12 minutes or until golden. Cool on wire racks.
Yield: 40 wafers

Shannon Tollison
Edgefield, SC

RUSSIAN TEA MIX

1 cup orange-flavored breakfast beverage crystals
½ cup sugar
¼ cup instant lemon-flavored tea
½ teaspoon ground cinnamon
¼ teaspoon ground cloves

Mix ingredients well. To serve, stir 2 teaspoons tea mix into 1 cup hot water.
Yield: about 2 cups mix

Elsie Morgan
Edgefield, SC

APPLE-SHERRY PUNCH

4 cups apple juice or cider, chilled
¼ cup lemon juice
1 cup sherry

Combine all ingredients. Pour into punch cups and serve immediately.
Yield: 6 to 8 servings

Ed Andrews
Williamston, NC

HOT FRUIT-WINE PUNCH

1½ cups apple juice
3 cinnamon sticks
12 whole cloves
3 tablespoons honey or sugar
3 slices lemon
1 (750 ml) bottle blush, rosé, or dry red wine

Boil apple juice and next 4 ingredients for 5 minutes. Strain. Add
wine, and heat, but do not boil. Serve hot in mugs.
Yield: 8 to 10 servings

Ed Andrews
Williamston, NC

SUMMER SLUSH PUNCH

4 cups sugar
13 cups water, divided
3 (3-ounce) boxes jello
2 (26-ounce) cans pineapple juice
3 (6-ounce) cans frozen lemonade, thawed
2 (16-ounce) bottles ginger ale or lemon–lime carbonated beverage

Boil 4 cups sugar in 4 cups water. Add jello and remaining water. Add
juice and undiluted lemonade. Stir. Pour into mixing bowl. Place into
freezer. Stir 3 times in first 4 hours. When ready to serve, pour into a
½ gallon container or punch bowl, add soda, and stir until mixed.
Yield: 16 to 18 servings

Lisa Walenga
Indianola, IA

The following 26 beverages were donated by Austin Nichols Distilling Co., Lawrenceburg, KY

TURKEY JULEP

2 mint sprigs
2 ounces Wild Turkey Liqueur

Bruise a mint sprig in the bottom of a silver cup. Fill with crushed ice. Add liqueur. Serve with straws. Garnish with mint.
Yield: 1 serving

SWEET TURKEY

2 ounces Wild Turkey Liqueur
2 ounces Wild Turkey Bourbon

Place ice cubes in a rocks glass. Add liqueur and bourbon. Stir to blend.
Yield: 1 serving

ALEXANDER THE GREAT

1 ounce Wild Turkey Liqueur
1 ounce brandy
3 ounces vanilla ice cream
Chocolate sprinkles (optional)

Into blender, add liqueur, brandy, and ice cream, and blend until creamy. Pour into a wine goblet. Garnish with chocolate sprinkles if desired.
Yield: 1 serving

TURKEY EGG

2 ounces Wild Turkey Liqueur
6 ounces orange juice
1 raw egg or ¼ cup egg substitute

Into blender, add all ingredients, and process at high speed until smooth. Pour over ice.
Yield: 2 servings

THE PILGRIM

1½ ounce Wild Turkey Liqueur
Cranberry juice
1 orange or lemon wedge

Place ice cubes into a tall glass. Add liqueur. Fill with cranberry juice. Garnish with orange or lemon wedge.
Yield: 1 serving

WILD TURKEY CRIMSON SOUR

1½ ounces Wild Turkey 101
1½ ounces grenadine
3 ounces sweet & sour mix
1 orange slice
1 maraschino cherry

Shake or quickly blend first 3 ingredients with cracked ice. Pour into tall glass. Garnish with fruit.
Yield: 1 serving

TURKEY TWIST

¾ ounce Wild Turkey 101
¾ ounce triple sec
1½ ounces sweet & sour mix
Lemon-lime carbonated drink
1 lime peel twist

Shake or blend first 3 ingredients with cracked ice. Pour into a tall glass. Fill with soda, and stir. Garnish with a lime twist.
Yield: 1 serving

THE CITRUS TURKEY

1½ ounces Wild Turkey 101
1 ounce club soda
1 ounce orange juice
1 orange slice
1 lemon quarter

Fill large rocks glass with ice cubes. Add Wild Turkey 101, and next 2 ingredients. Stir. Garnish with orange slice. Squeeze lemon slightly and drop into drink.
Yield: 1 serving

WILD TURKEY MANHATTAN

2 ounces Wild Turkey 101
1 ounce sweet vermouth
Dash of angostura bitters
1 maraschino cherry

Fill mixing glass half full of cracked ice. Add Wild Turkey 101, and next 2 ingredients. Stir. Strain drink into a chilled Manhattan or martini glass. Garnish with cherry.
Yield: 1 serving

WILD TURKEY SOUR

1½ ounces Wild Turkey 101
3 ounces sweet & sour mix
Club soda
1 orange slice
1 maraschino cherry

Add Wild Turkey 101, sweet & sour mix, and cracked ice into a mixing glass. Fill with soda. Place cup over the glass, shake well, and strain into a sour glass. Garnish with fruit.
Yield: 1 serving

WILD TURKEY OLD FASHIONED

2 maraschino cherries, divided
2 orange peel twists, divided
¾ ounce simple syrup
2 ounces Wild Turkey 101
½ ounce dry vermouth
½ ounce sweet & sour mix
Dash of angostura bitters

In a mixing cup, crush 1 cherry and 1 orange peel twist in simple syrup. Add remaining ingredients, cover with mixing cup, and shake briefly. Pour into an ice–filled old–fashioned glass. Garnish with remaining fruit.
Yield: 1 serving

TURKEY COLLINS

1¼ ounces Wild Turkey 101
3 ounces sweet & sour mix
Splash of club soda
1 maraschino cherry
1 orange slice
1 lemon slice

Into a shaker, mix Wild Turkey 101, sweet & sour mix, and club soda. Strain into an ice-filled collins glass. Garnish with fruit.
Yield: 1 serving

WILD TURKEY PRESBYTERIAN

1½ ounces Wild Turkey 101
Ginger ale
Club soda
1 lemon peel twist

Pour Wild Turkey 101 into a tall, ice-filled glass. Add equal parts ginger ale and club soda, and stir gently. Garnish with lemon twist.
Yield: 1 serving

WILD TURKEY MINT JULEP

2 to 3 mint sprigs
1 teaspoon sugar
½ teaspoon water
1½ ounces Wild Turkey 101

Into a tall collins glass, add mint, sugar, and water. Stir until well blended. Fill with crushed ice and Wild Turkey 101. Stir until glass is well-frosted.
Yield: 1 serving

WILD TURKEY ORANGE FIZZ

1½ ounces Wild Turkey 101
Splash of orange juice
Club soda

Fill a tumbler with ice. Add Wild Turkey 101, orange juice, and top with club soda. Stir.
Yield: 1 serving

WILD TURKEY LIME FIZZ

1½ ounces Wild Turkey 101
Splash of Rose's lime juice
¼ lime
Club soda

Fill a tumbler with ice. Add Wild Turkey 101, Rose's lime juice, a squeeze of lime, and top with club soda. Stir.
Yield: 1 serving

WILD TURKEY LEMON FIZZ

1½ ounces Wild Turkey 101
1 lemon quarter
Club soda

Fill a tumbler with ice. Add Wild Turkey 101, a squeeze of lemon, and top with club soda. Stir.
Yield: 1 serving

WILD TURKEY AND ORANGE JUICE

1½ ounces Wild Turkey 101
Orange juice

Pour Wild Turkey 101 into an ice–filled goblet or tall glass. Fill with orange juice. Stir.
Yield: 1 serving

WILD ICED TEA

1½ ounces Wild Turkey 101
2½ ounces sweet & sour mix
Splash of triple sec
Cola
1 lemon slice

Pour Wild Turkey 101, sweet & sour mix, and triple sec into a tall, ice-filled glass. Fill with cola. Stir. Garnish with lemon.
Yield: 1 serving

WILD TURKEY GOBBLER

5½ ounces hot apple cider
1½ ounces Wild Turkey 101
1 cinnamon stick

Pour apple cider and Wild Turkey 101 into a mug. Stir. Garnish with cinnamon stick.
Yield: 1 serving

WILD TURKEY TODDY

2 ounces Wild Turkey 101
1 ounce orange juice
1 teaspoon sugar
1 whole clove
¼ pat butter

Place first four ingredients into a mug. Fill with boiling water and stir. Top with butter.
Yield: 1 serving

KENTUCKY COFFEE

1 ounce Wild Turkey 101
½ ounce Truffles Liqueur de Chocolat
Hot coffee
Drambuie
Whipped cream

Pour Wild Turkey 101 and Truffles chocolate liqueur into a mug. Fill with hot coffee. Stir. Float Drambuie, and top with whipped cream.
Yield: 1 serving

GOLDEN NAIL

¾ ounce Wild Turkey Liqueur
¾ ounce Scotch whisky

Pour Wild Turkey Liqueur and Scotch into an ice-filled rocks glass. Stir to blend.
Yield: 1 serving

BIRD OF PARADISE

1½ ounces Wild Turkey Liqueur
3 ounces coconut cream
3 ounces pineapple juice
½ cup crushed ice

Into blender, add Wild Turkey Liqueur, next two ingredients, and ice. Blend thoroughly. Pour into a tumbler.
Yield: 1 serving

WHITE TURKEY

1 ounce Wild Turkey Liqueur
1 ounce cream

Fill rocks glass with ice. Add Wild Turkey Liqueur and cream. Stir gently.
Yield: 1 serving

COLD TURKEY

1 ounce Wild Turkey Liqueur
½ ounce peach brandy
Juice of quartered lime
Club soda

Fill rocks glass with ice cubes. Add Wild Turkey Liqueur, brandy, and lime juice. Fill with club soda. Stir lightly.
Yield: 1 serving

WILD TURKEY SOUP

1 turkey carcass, meat removed and reserved
4 medium carrots
1 small cabbage
3 stalks celery
1 teaspoon salt
½ teaspoon pepper
½ teaspoon poultry seasoning
1 (16-ounce) package macaroni, cooked
Leftover stuffing and gravy (optional)

Break carcass into pieces and place in an 8-quart soup pot. Cover with cold water, about 4 to 5 quarts. Bring slowly to the boiling point. Remove film. Cover, and simmer 2 hours to loosen meat. When cool, remove meat, and set aside. Chop carrots, and next 2 ingredients in a food processor. Add chopped vegetables, salt, next 2 ingredients, and any remaining stuffing and gravy to the broth. Simmer 2 hours. Adjust seasonings. Add macaroni.
Best served the next day.
Yield: 8 to 10 servings

Rob Keck
Edgefield, SC

CREAMY DIJON TURKEY SOUP

1 cup chopped celery
1 cup thinly sliced onion
3 tablespoons margarine
1 large garlic clove, minced
3 tablespoons flour
½ teaspoon salt
¼ teaspoon white pepper
4 cups skim milk
¼ cup Dijon mustard
2 teaspoons reduced-sodium chicken bouillon granules
2 cups cubed cooked turkey
French bread (optional)

Sauté celery and onions in margarine over medium-high heat 5 to 6 minutes, or until celery is tender, and onion is golden. Add garlic, and sauté 2 minutes. Stir in flour, salt, and pepper, and cook 2 minutes. Remove pan from heat, and slowly add milk, stirring constantly. Return pan to medium-high heat, stir in mustard and bouillon. Cook, stirring constantly, for 5 to 8 minutes, or until mixture is thickened and bubbling. Stir in turkey, and heat 2 minutes. Serve with French bread.

This recipe is low in fat.
Yield: 6 servings

National Turkey Federation
Reston, VA

TURK'S GOBBLER SOUP

1 large onion, sliced
2 stalks celery, sliced
3 tablespoons margarine
3 tablespoons flour
Dash of salt
Dash of pepper
2 quarts turkey broth
2 medium potatoes, cubed
2 carrots, julienned
2 zucchini, julienned
1 (16-ounce) can whole kernel corn, drained
1 cup dry white wine
4 cups cubed cooked turkey
2 tablespoons chopped parsley (optional)

Sauté onion and celery in margarine until tender, about 5 to 6 minutes. Remove from heat. Stir in flour, salt, and pepper. Gradually stir in broth until well-blended. Heat, stirring constantly, until mixture boils. Add potato and carrot. Cover, and simmer until vegetables are barely tender, about 15 minutes. Add zucchini and remaining ingredients. Simmer 15 minutes more.
Serve topped with parsley.
Yield: 8 to 10 servings

Mike Halter
East Ridge, TN

TURKEY MEATBALL CHOWDER

1 medium onion, chopped
1 garlic clove, minced
1 tablespoon vegetable oil
1 cup water
4 (16-ounce) cans whole tomatoes, chopped, undrained
1 (15-ounce) can pinto or kidney beans, undrained
1 tablespoon Worcestershire sauce
2 teaspoons dried basil, crushed
¼ teaspoon salt
¼ teaspoon pepper

MEATBALLS

1 pound ground turkey
½ cup finely crushed saltines
¼ cup Parmesan cheese
½ teaspoon dried thyme, crushed
6 cups finely chopped cabbage

In a large saucepan, sauté onion and garlic in oil until tender. Add water and next 6 ingredients. Bring to a boil, reduce heat. Simmer, covered, for 2 hours. For meatballs, combine turkey and next 3 ingredients. Shape into 36 meatballs. Bake in 375° oven for 15 minutes. Drain on paper towels. Add meatballs and cabbage to soup. Simmer, covered, for 20 minutes.
Yield: 8 to 10 servings

David Cleveland
Tullahoma, TN

28

WILD TURKEY GUMBO

1 cup flour
1 cup olive oil
4 quarts turkey broth
1½ bunches green onions, chopped
1 large red or yellow bell pepper, diced
1 stalk celery, diced
1½ cloves garlic, minced
2½ teaspoons pepper
¾ teaspoon cayenne pepper
2½ teaspoons paprika
2½ teaspoons salt
¾ teaspoon chili powder
1 bay leaf
8 cups cubed turkey breast
½ pound smoked deer or pork sausage, cubed

Make roux by blending flour and oil in a heavy saucepan over medium heat, stirring constantly for 30 to 45 minutes until chocolate in color. Do not leave unattended or it will burn. Set aside to cool. Remove excess oil from top, and reserve. Gradually add roux to broth; bring to a slow boil. In oil reserved from roux, sauté vegetables until tender. Add seasonings, turkey cubes, and vegetables into boiling broth. Brown deer or pork sausage in skillet. Drain. Add to soup pot and cook 1 hour.
Serve over steamed rice.
Yield: 16 (12-ounce) servings

Dale Bounds
Lufkin, TX

WILD TURKEY GUMBO SOUP

1 turkey carcass
1 large onion, chopped
5 celery tops
1½ teaspoons salt
¼ teaspoon pepper
¼ teaspoon herb seasoning blend
2 chicken bouillon cubes
2 quarts water
2 cups fresh or frozen okra
2 (16-ounce) cans whole tomatoes
½ cup rice

Place turkey carcass and next six ingredients into a soup pot. Cover with water. Bring to a boil. Remove film. Cover and simmer for 2 hours. Remove carcass. When cool, remove any meat from carcass, and reserve. Strain. Discard solids. Return broth to pot, add turkey and remaining ingredients, and bring to boil. Reduce heat, cover, and cook until rice is done, about 30 minutes. Adjust seasoning to taste.
Yield: 12 servings

Debbie LeCroy
Bradley, SC

ERICA'S POTATO SOUP

1 cup finely diced celery
½ cup finely diced onion
1 tablespoon butter
4 cups russet potatoes, peeled and cubed
3 cups water
1 pint half-and-half
½ teaspoon salt
¼ teaspoon pepper

In a 3-quart saucepan over medium-high heat, sauté celery and onion in butter until soft. Add potatoes and water. Bring to a boil. Cover. Reduce to a simmer; cook until potatoes are soft, about 15 minutes. Remove potatoes. Mash coarsely. Add half-and-half, salt, and pepper to taste. Stir potatoes into celery-onion mixture. Heat thoroughly.
Yield: 4 servings

Erica Welker
Lacey, WA

MIDWESTERN CHEDDAR CHEESE SOUP

2 quarts turkey stock
1 quart milk
3 pounds Cheddar cheese, shredded
1 tablespoon vegetable oil
1 medium onion, diced
5 stalks celery, chopped
2 carrots, grated
1 tablespoon dry mustard
4 teaspoons Tabasco sauce
1 teaspoon Worcestershire sauce

ROUX

2½ sticks butter
1 cup plus 2 tablespoons flour
Minced chives (optional)
Croutons (optional)

Bring turkey stock and next 2 ingredients to near boiling, stirring to incorporate cheese. Heat oil in skillet. Cook onion and next 2 ingredients until softened. Stir in dry mustard and next 2 ingredients. Cool. Purée flavorings in food processor or blender. In skillet, stir butter and flour constantly until incorporated to form roux. Do not brown. Stir in 2 cups turkey broth; then add slowly into soup pot until desired thickness is reached.

Hint: Garnish with minced chives or croutons if desired.
Yield: 8 to 10 servings

James Earl and Mary Kennamer
Edgefield, SC

WILD RICE SOUP

3 cups canned chicken broth
2 cups water
1 cup wild rice
½ cup chopped green onions
½ cup butter
½ cup flour
2 cups milk or half-and-half
¼ teaspoon poultry seasoning
½ teaspoon salt
½ teaspoon pepper
6 slices bacon, cubed
2 cups cooked turkey, cubed
½ cup minced parsley

In large saucepan, bring chicken broth and next 3 ingredients to a boil. Reduce heat and simmer 40 minutes. In a medium saucepan, melt butter over moderate heat. Stir in flour, and cook until bubbly. Remove pan from heat. Gradually whisk in milk or half-and-half; add poultry seasoning and next 2 ingredients. Cook until thickened. Stir into broth. Fry bacon until crisp. Drain. Add bacon and turkey to broth. Cook 2 to 3 minutes, or until bubbling. Ladle into bowls. Top with parsley.
Yield: 6 servings

LaVerne Vincent
Fort Lauderdale, FL

FIVE ONION SOUP

½ stick butter
3 shallots, minced
1 small onion, chopped
1 small red onion, chopped
2 green onions, chopped
1 leek, white and pale green parts only, chopped
1 tablespoon minced garlic
⅛ teaspoon ground cloves
4 cups canned beef broth
⅔ cup dry sherry
Pinch of salt

GARLIC BUTTER

2 tablespoons butter, melted
1 teaspoon minced garlic

CROUTONS

4 slices French bread, cut ½ inch thick
½ cup Parmesan cheese, freshly grated

GARNISH

4 slices Swiss cheese
4 slices mozzarella cheese

Melt butter in heavy Dutch oven over medium-high heat. Add shallots, and next 4 ingredients. Sauté until golden, about 15 minutes. Add garlic and cloves. Cook 1 minute. Stir in broth and sherry. Bring to boil. Reduce heat to medium-low, cover, and simmer 30 minutes. Add salt to taste. Preheat broiler. Combine butter and garlic in small bowl. Place bread on baking sheet and brush with half of garlic butter. Broil bread until lightly browned; turn and repeat process. Sprinkle with Parmesan cheese. Ladle soup into crocks. Top each with crouton. Bake until soup is bubbling and cheese is melted and golden, about 10 minutes.

Can be prepared 1 day ahead, covered, and refrigerated.
Yield: 4 servings

Erica Welker
Lacey, WA

33

HOMEMADE ROLLS

1 (¼-ounce) package active dry yeast
½ cup lukewarm water
⅔ cup shortening
⅔ cup sugar
2 teaspoons salt
1 cup hot mashed potatoes
1 cup hot potato water
3 eggs, beaten
7 cups unbleached all-purpose flour, divided
½ stick melted butter

Dissolve yeast in water. Place shortening and next 4 ingredients in a large mixing bowl. Stir until shortening and sugar melt. Cool mixture to lukewarm. Stir in eggs. Mix in 2 cups flour. Blend in yeast mixture. Knead in remaining flour until dough is smooth and can be handled easily. Transfer dough to lightly greased bowl, cover, and allow to rise until doubled in size, about 2 hours. Punch dough down, cover, and refrigerate at least 8 hours, or overnight. Roll out dough with rolling pin. Cut into 72 rolls shaped as desired. Place in lightly greased pan, cover, and let rise until doubled in size, about 1½ to 2 hours. Bake at 400° for 10-12 minutes, or until lightly browned. Brush tops with melted butter.
Rolls freeze well.
Yield: 72 rolls

Susan Fowler
Tullahoma, TN

GRANDMA'S REFRIGERATOR ROLLS

1 cup sugar
3 cups boiling water
2 tablespoons butter
1 tablespoon salt
2 eggs, beaten
8 to 9 cups all-purpose flour, divided
2 (¼-ounce) packages active dry yeast
½ cup warm water

Mix sugar and next 3 ingredients. Let mixture cool. Stir in eggs and 2 cups flour. In small well-greased bowl, dissolve yeast in water, and add to the other mixture. Stir in 4 cups flour. Add remaining flour and knead until smooth and elastic. Cover, set in warm place, and let rise until doubled, about 1½ to 2 hours. Punch dough down. Form into rolls. Cover, and let rise again. Bake at 350° for 20-25 minutes.
Yield: 4 to 5 dozen

Mary Kay Coffey
Walden, IA

THANKSGIVING DAY ROLLS

1 (¼-ounce) package active dry yeast
3 tablespoons sugar, divided
1 cup warm water
1 cup warm milk
1 scant tablespoon salt
3 to 4 cups all-purpose flour, divided
2 tablespoons margarine, melted

Stir yeast and 1 tablespoon sugar into water. Let stand for 5 minutes. Empty into large bowl, and stir in milk, salt, and remaining sugar. Add 2 cups flour; then continue to add flour until dough is right consistency for kneading. Turn onto lightly floured board, and knead until dough is smooth and elastic. Transfer to greased bowl. Cover, and let rise until doubled in bulk. Punch down and let rise again until doubled. Form dough into rolls. Place in lightly greased pan. Bake at 400° for 15 minutes or until golden. Brush tops with melted margarine. Cool.
Yield: 3 to 4 dozen

Ivy Coffey
Russell, IA

EASY CORNBREAD

1¼ cups all-purpose flour
¾ cup cornmeal
¼ cup sugar
2 teaspoons baking powder
½ teaspoon salt
1 cup skim milk
¼ cup vegetable oil
2 egg whites or 1 egg, beaten

Combine flour and next 4 ingredients. Stir in milk, oil, and egg whites, mixing just enough to moisten dry ingredients. Pour into greased 9x9-inch pan. Bake at 400° for 20 to 25 minutes, or until golden and wooden toothpick inserted near center comes out clean. Serve warm.
Yield: 6 to 8 servings

Missouri Egg Merchandising Council
Columbia, MO

YUMMY BISCUITS

1 (¼-ounce) package active dry yeast
1¼ cups room temperature milk, divided
3½ cups all-purpose flour, divided
4½ teaspoons baking powder
1 teaspoon sugar
¾ teaspoon salt
⅓ cup shortening, chilled

Dissolve yeast in ¼ cup warm milk. Sift 3 cups flour and next 3 ingredients into a large bowl. Cut in shortening with a pastry blender until mixture resembles coarse meal. Stir in yeast mixture and remaining milk. Turn dough onto lightly floured board and knead gently, 10 to 12 times. Roll dough to ½ inch thickness. Dip biscuit cutter into remaining flour and cut straight down without twisting. Place biscuits on ungreased cookie sheet. Cover with cloth, and let rise for 15 minutes. Bake at 450° for 12 to 15 minutes, or until golden.
Yield: 12 large or 24 small biscuits

Lynn Coffey
Love, VA

PEANUT BUTTER AND JELLY BREAD

1 (¼-ounce) package active dry yeast
¼ cup warm water
Pinch of sugar
1½ cups apple juice
½ cup peanut butter
3 tablespoons brown sugar
3 tablespoons vegetable oil
1 teaspoon salt
5 cups all-purpose flour, divided
6 tablespoons jelly, any flavor, divided

Dissolve yeast in water and sugar. Let stand about 10 minutes, until foaming. In medium saucepan, heat apple juice and next 4 ingredients and beat together until peanut butter melts. Cool to room temperature. Transfer peanut butter mixture to large bowl, and incorporate 2 cups flour. Add enough flour to form dough that can be easily kneaded. Knead 8 to 10 minutes. Transfer to greased bowl. Cover. Let rise until doubled in bulk. Punch down and divide into 2 portions. Roll out and spread 3 tablespoons jelly on each. Roll up each dough length and place in loaf pan. Cover. Let rise until doubled in size. Bake at 375° for 35 minutes.
Yield: 2 loaves

Mary Harris
Makanda, IA

KRINGLE
(NORWEGIAN SWEET BISCUIT)

1 cup sugar
1¼ sticks margarine, divided
1 egg
1 cup buttermilk
1 teaspoon baking soda
2 teaspoons baking powder
3 to 5 cups all–purpose flour, divided

Cream sugar, 1 stick margarine, and egg. Blend buttermilk, next 2 ingredients, and 3 cups flour. Cool in refrigerator. Use remaining flour to make dough stiff enough to roll. Roll small amount into long strip and form Figure 8 about 5 inches tall. Continue with remaining dough. Bake on cookie sheet 10 to 15 minutes at 475° until golden. Melt remaining margarine, and brush top when out of oven.
Yield: 12 to 18 servings

Sandy Piatt
Madrid, IA

CHRISTMAS MORNING
SWEET ROLLS

1 (8-count) package homestyle rolls dough balls
1 (3-ounce) package pudding mix, any flavor, not instant
¼ cup brown sugar
1 stick butter, melted
½ cup chopped pecans, optional

Roll dough into 1-inch balls; set aside. In small bowl, combine pudding mix and brown sugar. Roll dough balls in melted butter then in pudding mixture. Place in bottom of a Bundt pan; continue to layer. Top with nuts, if desired. Leave at room temperature at least 8 hours or overnight. Bake at 350° for 30 to 35 minutes until brown. Invert onto plate.
Yield: 8 servings

Diana Showalter
Roann, IN

PUMPKIN BREAD

3½ cups all-purpose flour
1½ teaspoons salt
1 teaspoon cinnamon
1 teaspoon nutmeg
2 teaspoons baking soda
3 cups sugar
1 cup vegetable oil
4 eggs
1 (16-ounce) can pumpkin
⅔ cup water
2 tablespoons sesame seeds

Combine flour and next 4 ingredients. In large bowl, mix sugar and next 3 ingredients. Add water, and mix well. Add dry ingredients and sesame seeds into pumpkin mixture. Grease and flour two loaf pans. Bake at 350° for about 60 minutes, or until loaf pulls slightly from sides and is springy to the touch. Let stand 10 minutes; then turn out on a wire rack to cool before slicing.

To make banana bread, substitute 2 cups mashed bananas for pumpkin and 1 cup chopped walnuts for sesame seeds.

Yield: 2 loaves

Nancy Hewitt
Mexico, IN

Nothing succeeds like success. From an obscure beginning in 1973, the National Wild Turkey Federation has experienced fantastic growth to become one of the largest wildlife conservation organizations in America. Its future holds even greater promise. Volunteers across our nation and beyond have played a key role in making it happen. Our emphasis on God, country, the flag, and the conservation ethic is the catalyst for this amazing success.

Earl Groves
Gastonia, NC

SPOON BREAD

1 cup cornmeal, sifted
3 cups milk
1½ teaspoons salt
2 tablespoons butter
3 eggs, separated
1 tablespoon sugar

In a Dutch oven on low heat, combine the cornmeal and next 2 ingredients until thickened, stirring constantly. Remove from stove and cool slightly. Add butter, egg yolks, and sugar into cornmeal mixture, and mix well. Beat egg whites, and fold into mixture. Place into a greased and preheated 13x9x2-inch rectangular pan. Place in 375° oven, immediately turn down temperature to 350°, and bake for 30 minutes.
Yield: 6 servings

ON THE SIDE...OR IN THE BIRD

Salads, Side Dishes, Stuffings

To be a volunteer working for the wild turkey and being a part of the National Wild Turkey Federation, the greatest conservation organization in the country, is exciting. The opportunity to work with the staff, the employees, and the volunteers of the NWTF, who are so dedicated to the resource, has given me great pleasure, along with the opportunity to meet many new friends.

As a volunteer, we are the heart of the NWTF. To see populations of wild turkeys increasing to an estimated four million, and membership increasing from 40,000 to 120,000 in the nine years I have been a volunteer, makes for a "healthy heart."

If you accept the challenge of becoming a volunteer, you will find the wild turkey and the NWTF are synonymous with excitement and challenge.

Gary G. VanDyke,
Vicksburg, MI

FRUITED TURKEY SALAD

4 cups cubed cooked turkey
1½ cups seedless green grapes, halved
1 cup canned tidbit pineapple, drained
1 cup diced celery
¾ cup mayonnaise
¼ cup lemon juice concentrate
1 teaspoon ground ginger
½ teaspoon salt
Lettuce leaves
½ cup chopped cashews or walnuts

In large bowl, combine turkey and next 3 ingredients. In small bowl, combine mayonnaise and next 3 ingredients, and pour over turkey mixture. Mix well. Cover and chill at least 1 hour before serving. Line lettuce leaves on plates. Top with turkey salad sprinkled with nuts.
Yield: 4 servings

TURKEY STRAWBERRY SPINACH SALAD

8 cups spinach leaves, washed and torn into bite-size pieces
½ pound fresh asparagus, blanched and cut into 1-inch pieces
1 (2¼-ounce) can sliced black olives
3 eggs, hard-boiled, quartered
2 cups strawberries, hulled and sliced
2 cups diced cooked turkey breast
1 cup white or red seedless grapes, halved

VINAIGRETTE

1 tablespoon red or white wine vinegar
⅛ teaspoon salt
⅛ teaspoon white pepper
6 tablespoons olive oil
1 tablespoons fresh orange juice
1 tablespoon orange zest
2 tablespoons poppy or sesame seeds

Layer, from bottom to top, spinach and next 6 ingredients, in large
glass bowl. In a medium bowl, beat vinegar with salt and pepper.
Drizzle in oil, whisking constantly. Whisk in remaining ingredients.
Toss salad with vinaigrette, and serve immediately.
Yield: 6 to 8 servings

Missouri Poultry Federation
Columbia, MO

43

ROASTED SOUTHWESTERN TURKEY SALAD WITH ANCHO-HONEY DRESSING

2 cups cooked roasted turkey, julienned
¼ cup carrots, julienned
¼ cup zucchini, julienned
¼ cup yellow squash, julienned
½ cup red bell pepper, julienned
¼ cup red onion, julienned
½ cup cooked black beans, drained
½ cup roasted or frozen corn kernels
1 head Boston lettuce, washed and torn into bite-size pieces

CILANTRO MAYONNAISE

½ cup cilantro, chopped
1 egg yolk
1 tablespoon Dijon mustard
1 shallot, minced
1 garlic clove, minced
1 serrano chile, minced
1½ tablespoons lime juice
1½ cups vegetable oil
Salt, as needed

TORTILLA STRIPS

3 corn tortillas, halved
1 cup vegetable oil

ANCHO-HONEY DRESSING

3 ancho chiles, seeded
2 shallots, chopped
2 garlic cloves, chopped
¼ cup cilantro, chopped
1½ cups water
⅓ cup honey
¼ cup white wine vinegar
½ cup vegetable oil
1½ tablespoons lime juice
Salt, as needed

Combine turkey, carrot, and next 6 ingredients; set aside. For mayonnaise, process cilantro and next 6 ingredients in a food processor. Slowly add oil until incorporated; add salt and set aside. Cut tortillas into thin strips. Heat oil to 350°. Fry strips until crisp.

Drain on paper towels. For dressing, simmer anchos and next 4 ingredients on medium heat until reduced by two-thirds, about 10 minutes. Pour into a blender and purée until smooth. Add honey and vinegar, running until incorporated. Add oil in a thin stream. When incorporated, add lime juice and salt to taste. Add enough cilantro mayonnaise to the turkey mixture to coat. Toss lettuce in some of the dressing, and place on a chilled plate to form a well. Top with the turkey mixture. Garnish with tortilla strips.
Yield: 4 to 6 servings

Kirk Williams
Sacramento, CA

TURKEY SALAD

1 cup chopped cooked turkey
¼ cup mayonnaise or mayonnaise-type salad dressing
2 eggs, hard-boiled, peeled and chopped
1 tablespoon chopped sweet or dill pickles
Salt, as needed
Pepper, as needed

Combine all ingredients.
Divide into portions and serve on beds of lettuce.
Yield: 4 servings

Debbie LeCroy
Bradley, SC

YUMMY TURKEY SALAD

2½ cups cooked diced turkey
1 cup diced Red Delicious apple, unpeeled
1 cup diced celery
½ cup golden raisins
1 teaspoon lemon juice
¾ cup mayonnaise
Dash of lemon pepper

Mix all ingredients in bowl. Cover. Refrigerate at least 2 hours.
Serve over Boston lettuce leaves, and top with chopped pecans if desired.
Yield: 4 servings

Kris Gardner
Harpersville, AL

In the last three years, the National Wild Turkey Federation has donated more than $105,000 to ensure the future of the American hunting heritage. Some of the organizations that your money has gone to are the Wildlife Legislative Fund of America, the Governor's Symposium on the American Hunting Heritage, The Congressional Sportsmen's Caucus, and the Wildlife Partners Network. The National Wild Turkey Federation will continue to do all it can to preserve the wild turkey hunting tradition.

Lynn Boykin
Mobile, AL
1995-96 President, NWTF

HOT TURKEY SALAD

1 cup cream of chicken soup
1 cup mayonnaise
3 cups cooked chopped wild turkey
1 cup chopped celery
1 (13.25-ounce) can mushroom stems and pieces, drained
1 cup grated Cheddar cheese
1 cup slivered almonds
Nonstick cooking spray
4 to 6 toasted buns

Mix soup with mayonnaise. Add turkey and next 4 ingredients. Coat a 2-quart casserole with nonstick cooking spray. Transfer turkey mixture to casserole. Bake at 350° for 30 to 40 minutes. Serve on buns.
Yield: 4 servings

TURKEY SALAD WITH VINAIGRETTE DRESSING

2 tablespoons white wine vinegar
1 tablespoon olive oil
2 tablespoons lime juice
¼ teaspoon salt
¼ teaspoon pepper
¼ teaspoon ground ginger
¼ cup minced red onion
1 jalapeño pepper, seeded and minced
1 pound cooked no-salt turkey breast, cubed
4 leaves red leaf lettuce

In medium bowl, whisk vinegar and next 5 ingredients. Stir in onion, jalapeño, and turkey. Cover and refrigerate at least 4 hours. Line plates with lettuce. Spoon salad on top.
Yield: 4 servings

Iowa Turkey Federation
Ames, IA

TURKEY CURRY SALAD

¾ cup mayonnaise
¾ cup sour cream or plain yogurt
1½ teaspoons curry powder
4 cups diced cooked turkey
2 cups chopped apple
1 cup chopped celery
1 cup chopped, peeled cucumber
2 tablespoons chopped onion

In a large bowl, combine mayonnaise with sour cream or yogurt. Stir in curry powder. Fold in remaining ingredients. Chill at least 2 hours before serving.
This makes a pretty luncheon main course served on croissants or stuffed in tomatoes.
Yield: 6 to 8 servings

Mary Jo Burke
Westby, WI

BLUEBERRY SALAD

1 (8-ounce) can crushed pineapple, drained, juice reserved
1 (21-ounce) can blueberry pie filling
2 (3-ounce) packages blueberry or black cherry gelatin

TOPPING

1 (8-ounce) package cream cheese, softened
1 (8-ounce) carton sour cream
½ cup sugar
½ teaspoon vanilla
½ cup chopped nuts

In medium bowl, mix pineapple with pie filling. In another bowl, dissolve gelatin in reserved pineapple juice and enough boiling water to equal 3 cups liquid. Stir pineapple-blueberry mixture into jello-pineapple juice mixture. Pour into an 11x7x1½-inch rectangular pan. Chill in refrigerator 2 to 3 hours to set before making and spreading on the topping and nuts. In medium bowl, combine cream cheese and next 3 ingredients. Spread on top of blueberry mixture. Sprinkle with nuts. Refrigerate until firm.
Yield: 8 servings

Debbie LeCroy
Bradley, SC

KELLI'S ORANGE SALAD

1 (6-ounce) package orange gelatin
2 cups boiling water
1½ cups cold water
1 (11-ounce) can mandarin oranges, drained
1 (8-ounce) can crushed pineapple
1 (16-ounce) carton small-curd cottage cheese
1 (8-ounce) container frozen whipped topping

Combine gelatin with water. Pour into a 9¼x2¾-inch ring mold. Cool until set. In medium bowl, combine oranges and remaining ingredients. Spoon orange mixture into mold. Refrigerate until firm.
Yield: 6 to 8 servings

Kelli Showalter
Roann, IN

EVELINA'S WALDORF SALAD

2 cups diced unpeeled Golden Delicious apples
1 cup diced celery
⅓ cup chopped nuts
½ cup mayonnaise
3 tablespoons whipped cream
Maraschino cherries (optional)

Combine all ingredients. Garnish with cherries if desired.
Yield: 4 to 6 servings

Rick Fields
Tucson, AZ

RASPBERRY-WINE SALAD

1 (6-ounce) package raspberry gelatin
2 cups boiling water
1 (16-ounce) can whole-berry cranberry sauce
½ cup dry red wine
1 (8-ounce) can crushed pineapple, undrained
⅓ cup chopped walnuts

CHEESE FLUFF DRESSING

1 cup frozen whipped topping, thawed
1 (3-ounce) package cream cheese, softened
3 tablespoons milk
½ teaspoon orange zest

Dissolve gelatin into boiling water. Add cranberry sauce, stirring until
sauce melts. Stir in wine. Chill until the consistency of an unbeaten
egg white. Fold in pineapple and walnuts. Spoon mixture into a lightly
oiled 8-cup ring mold. Cover with foil. Chill until firm. For dressing,
beat all ingredients with electric mixer until well blended. Serve
dressing with salad.
Yield: 6 to 8 servings

Dottie McGirt
Lexington, NC

FROZEN CRANBERRY SALAD

½ (3-ounce) package cream cheese, softened
1 tablespoon mayonnaise or light sour cream
1 teaspoon lemon juice
1 (8-ounce) container frozen whipped topping, thawed
1 (16-ounce) can whole-berry cranberry sauce
1 (20-ounce) can crushed pineapple, drained
½ cup pecan pieces
Lettuce leaves
Frozen whipped topping

Mix first 7 ingredients together. Freeze in muffin tins or in a loaf pan sprayed with cooking spray. Serve on lettuce leaves and dollop with frozen whipped topping.
Yield: 8 servings

Susan Fowler
Tullahoma, TN

CRANBERRY TREAT

1 (16-ounce) bag cranberries, washed and picked over
2 oranges, peeled and seeded
6 red apples, unpeeled and cored
1 (8-ounce) can crushed pineapple, drained
3 cups sugar
1 cup chopped nuts

Pulse cranberries and next 2 ingredients in food processor, and grind until chunky. Stir in pineapple and remaining ingredients. Chill at least 8 hours before serving.
Yield: 8 to 10 servings

Linda Rosenlieb
Edgefield, SC

CALIFORNIA SALAD

1 cup torn fresh spinach
4 cups torn romaine
1 cup torn red leaf lettuce
1 (11-ounce) can mandarin oranges, drained
1 red onion, thinly sliced
1 (2-ounce) package slivered almonds

GARLIC DRESSING

5 tablespoons vegetable oil
2 tablespoons vinegar
1 teaspoon garlic salt
1 small garlic clove, crushed
⅛ teaspoon pepper

Toss salad greens. Top with oranges and next 2 ingredients. In small bowl, whisk together all ingredients. Let stand for 15 minutes. Strain off garlic. Pour dressing over salad. Toss. Serve immediately.
Yield: 6 servings

Diana Showalter
Roann, IN

LITTLE WABASH OVERNIGHT SALAD

1 head iceberg lettuce, torn into pieces
1 head cauliflower, cut up
1 bell pepper, chopped
1 bunch green onions, chopped
1 pound bacon, fried and crumbled

RANCH DRESSING

1 (1-ounce) package ranch-style dressing mix
1 cup mayonnaise
1 cup milk

TOPPING

½ cup Parmesan cheese
½ (8-ounce) package shredded mild Cheddar cheese

Layer lettuce and next 4 ingredients. Combine dressing mix with mayonnaise and milk. Pour over salad. Top with cheeses. Refrigerate 12 to 24 hours. Toss before serving.
Yield: 6 to 8 servings

Marge Shubert
Watson, IL

MAGGIE RYDMAN'S SPINACH SALAD

1 pound fresh spinach, washed, stems removed
2 cups bean sprouts
1 (8-ounce) can sliced water chestnuts, drained
¼ cup chopped green onions
½ pound bacon, fried and crumbled
1 cup sliced mushrooms

DRESSING

¼ cup white wine vinegar
¼ cup vegetable oil
⅓ cup ketchup
2 teaspoons salt
⅓ cup + 2 tablespoons sugar
1 teaspoon Worcestershire sauce

Place spinach and next 5 ingredients in salad bowl. Add vinegar and next 5 ingredients into a jar. Shake. Toss salad with dressing.
Yield: 6 servings

Erica Welker
Lacey, WA

SMOKED GOUDA AND PENNE PASTA SALAD

1 (16-ounce) package penne pasta
1 (7-ounce) jar roasted peppers
10 cups fresh spinach, chopped
8 ounces smoked Gouda cheese
4 ounces provolone cheese, julienned
½ pound bacon, fried and crumbled

DRESSING

6 tablespoons olive oil
4 tablespoons vegetable oil
4 tablespoons cider vinegar
2 teaspoons minced garlic
Pinch of salt
Pinch of pepper
½ cup Parmesan cheese, freshly grated
6 drops Tabasco sauce

Cook penne. Drain, cool, and place in large bowl. Add roasted peppers and next 4 ingredients. Put dressing ingredients into a jar, cover tightly, and shake well. Pour over pasta salad. Mix well. Sprinkle with bacon.
Yield: 10 to 12 servings

Erica Welker
Lacey, WA

PRETZEL SALAD

2⅔ cups pretzels
1 stick butter, melted
1 (8-ounce) package cream cheese, softened
1 cup sugar
1 (8-ounce) container frozen whipped topping
2 (3-ounce) packages strawberry jello
2 cups boiling water
2 (10-ounce) packages frozen strawberries, thawed

Crush pretzels and place in 13x9x2-inch rectangular pan. Pour butter over pretzels. Bake at 350° for 20 minutes. Cool. Mix cream cheese with next 2 ingredients. Spread on pretzels. Dissolve jello in boiling water. Cool in refrigerator. Stir strawberries into jello. Pour jello mixture into pan. Refrigerate until congealed.
Yield: 8 to 10 servings

Susie Brown
Edgefield, SC

MIXED BEAN SALAD

1 (11-ounce) can white shoepeg corn, drained
1 (8.5-ounce) can small, young peas, drained
1 (15-ounce) can black-eyed peas, drained
1 (13.25-ounce) can baby lima beans, drained

DRESSING

1 cup vinegar
½ cup vegetable oil
½ onion, minced
½ cup sugar or 3 packages sugar substitute
1 teaspoon salt

Mix vegetables together in large bowl. Shake dressing ingredients in jar. Pour dressing over vegetables. Stir. Refrigerate at least 4 hours.
Keeps 1 week in refrigerator.
Yield: 10 to 12 servings

Susie Brown
Edgefield, SC

GUACAMOLE SALAD

2 large ripe avocados, peeled and pitted
1 medium onion, chopped
1 medium tomato, chopped
1 (8-ounce) package shredded mild Cheddar cheese
2 tablespoons mild salsa
1 teaspoon lemon juice

DIP

Sour cream
Salsa

Mash avocados with onion and tomatoes. Blend in cheese and next 2 ingredients. To make into a dip, add enough sour cream to the above mixture until it reaches a dip consistency. Add salsa to taste.
Yield: 4 to 6 servings

Sherry Haight
Mount Olive, MS

LAYERED SALAD

1 head iceberg lettuce, cut into bite-size pieces
3 carrots, shredded
½ onion, minced
1 (9-ounce) package frozen peas, cooked on High for 3 minutes in
  microwave
1 cup grated sharp Cheddar cheese
1 cup mayonnaise or mayonnaise-type salad dressing
½ cup sour cream
1 tablespoon milk
¼ cup Parmesan cheese

Layer lettuce and next 4 ingredients in large glass bowl. Mix mayonnaise with next 2 ingredients. Spoon over salad. Sprinkle Parmesan on top. Best made 1 day ahead.
Yield: 8 to 10 servings

Susie Brown
Edgefield, SC

CHEESY POTATO CASSEROLE

6 potatoes, unpeeled, cubed
½ pound bacon, fried and crumbled
½ pound processed cheese loaf
1 cup mayonnaise

Cook potato until tender. Transfer to a 3-quart casserole. Mix in
remaining ingredients. Chill 3 to 4 hours or overnight. Bake at 375°
uncovered for 30 to 40, until brown and bubbling.
Yield: 8 servings

Kelli Showalter
Roann, IN

MICROWAVED POTATO AND CHEESE CASSEROLE

1 stick butter or margarine, melted
1 (2-pound) package hash browns, partially thawed
1 cup chopped onion
½ cup sour cream
¾ teaspoon salt
1 (10¾-ounce) can condensed cream of chicken soup
2 cups grated Cheddar cheese, divided
Pinch of paprika

In a 3-quart casserole, add butter, potato, and next 4 ingredients. Top
with 1 cup cheese. Cook, covered, on High for 20 minutes. Stir once.
Sprinkle with remaining cheese and paprika. Cook 3 minutes on
High.
Yield: 10 to 12 servings

Jean Aikin
Hills, IA

SWEET POTATO CASSEROLE

4 medium sweet potatoes
1 cup sugar
1 stick margarine, softened
2 eggs
½ teaspoon salt
1 teaspoon vanilla
½ cup canned evaporated milk

TOPPING

1 cup brown sugar
1 cup chopped nuts
⅓ cup all-purpose flour
⅓ stick margarine, melted
1 teaspoon vanilla

Boil potatoes until tender, about 35-40 minutes. Cool. Peel and slice potatoes ¾ inch thick. In mixing bowl, cream sugar and margarine. Beat in eggs. Add salt, vanilla, and milk. Place potato in greased casserole. Pour mixture over potatoes. Mix together all topping ingredients, and crumble over potatoes. Bake at 350° for 35 minutes.
Yield: 4 to 6 servings

Rose Dameron
Lexington, NC

SWEET POTATO SOUFFLÉ

4 cups cooked sweet potato or 3 (28-ounce) cans
½ cup coconut (optional)
Dash of salt
2 eggs
1 cup sugar
⅓ cup butter, softened
1½ teaspoons vanilla
½ cup milk
1 cup chopped pecans
1 cup brown sugar
⅓ cup all-purpose flour
⅓ stick butter
1 cup crushed corn flakes

Mash sweet potatoes. Transfer to casserole. Add coconut, if desired, and next 6 ingredients. In medium bowl, combine pecans and remaining ingredients. Spread atop potatoes. Bake at 350° for 30 minutes.
Yield: 4 to 6 servings

Laura Terrell
Sherman, TX

SOUTHERN PEACH YAM BAKE

½ cup packed brown sugar
3 tablespoons flour
½ teaspoon nutmeg
2 tablespoons margarine
½ cup chopped pecans
2 (17-ounce) cans yams, drained
1 (16-ounce) can peach slices, drained
1½ cups miniature marshmallows

Combine sugar, flour, and nutmeg; cut in margarine until mixture resembles coarse crumbs. Add nuts. Arrange yams and peaches in 1½-quart casserole; sprinkle with sugar mixture. Bake at 350° for 35 minutes. Sprinkle with marshmallows. Broil until lightly browned.
Yield: 6 servings

Dottie McGirt
Lexington, NC

SPINACH PASTA

1 small onion, chopped
1 tablespoon minced garlic
2 tablespoons oil
1 (28-ounce) can whole tomatoes
1 (6-ounce) can tomato paste
2 teaspoons brown sugar
1 tablespoon oregano
1 tablespoon dried basil
2 (10-ounce) packages frozen chopped spinach, cooked and drained
1 (16-ounce) carton ricotta cheese
1 (8-ounce) package mozzarella cheese, grated
1 teaspoon salt
¼ teaspoon pepper
12 ounces large pasta shells, cooked

Sauté onion and garlic in oil. Cut up tomatoes. Add tomatoes and liquid to onion. Stir in tomato paste, sugar, oregano, and basil; bring to a boil. Reduce heat; simmer 20 minutes. In medium bowl, combine spinach and next 4 ingredients. Fill shells with spinach mixture and place in casserole. Pour sauce over shells. Bake at 350° for 30 minutes.
Yield: 4 servings

Laura Terrell
Sherman, TX

TURKEY FRIED RICE

¼ cup broccoli florets
¼ cup carrot, thinly sliced
¼ cup chopped green onions
¼ cup chopped celery
2 teaspoons vegetable oil
¼ cup sliced water chestnuts
¼ cup sliced mushrooms
¼ cup bean sprouts
¼ cup frozen sweet peas, partially thawed
1 cup rice, cooked
1 cup shredded cooked turkey
1½ tablespoons soy sauce
½ teaspoon sesame oil
½ teaspoon pepper
1 egg, beaten

In a large nonstick skillet or wok over medium-high heat, stir-fry broccoli and next 3 ingredients in oil for 1 to 2 minutes. Add water chestnuts and next 3 ingredients, and stir-fry 1 to 2 minutes more. Add rice and next 4 ingredients, and stir-fry 1 to 2 minutes, or until well-blended and hot. Make a well in center of turkey and rice mixture. Pour egg into well, and reduce heat to low; stir egg into turkey and rice mixture until egg is cooked.
Yield: 6 servings

National Turkey Federation
Reston, VA

BROWNED FRIED RICE

½ cup chopped onion
¾ cup rice
½ stick butter
1 (10½-ounce) can beef consommé
¾ soup can water
1 cup mushrooms (optional)

Brown onion and rice in butter, about 15 minutes. Place in covered 1½-quart casserole. Add remaining ingredients. Bake at 350° for 35 minutes or until browned and bubbling.
Yield: 4 servings

Allen Ricks
Morristown, TN

RICE CASSEROLE

1 cup instant rice
1 medium onion, chopped
1 stick margarine
1 (10¾-ounce) can cream of mushroom soup
1 (10¾-ounce) can chicken with rice soup
1 (7-ounce) can mushroom stems and pieces, drained
1 soup can water
Pinch of garlic powder

Brown rice and onion in margarine until golden. Transfer to baking dish. Mix soups and remaining ingredients and add to casserole. Bake at 350° for 30 minutes.
Yield: 4 servings

Linda Rosenlieb
Edgefield, SC

WILD RICE CASSEROLE

1 medium onion, chopped
1 medium bell pepper, chopped
¾ cup chopped celery
½ pound bacon, diced
½ pound mushrooms, sliced
6 cups cooked wild rice
1 cup frozen sweet peas (optional)
1 to 2 tablespoons soy sauce
¼ teaspoon pepper

In a large skillet, cook onion and next 3 ingredients until vegetables are tender, about 3 minutes. Add mushrooms. Cook for 2 minutes. Drain. Add rice and remaining ingredients. Cook, stirring gently, over moderate heat for 5 minutes.
Yield: 10 to 12 servings

Mary Jo Burke
Westby, WI

WILD RICE AND BROCCOLI CASSEROLE

1 (10-ounce) package frozen chopped broccoli
6 ounces wild rice, cooked
½ cup chopped onion
½ cup chopped celery
1 (10¾-ounce) can cream of chicken soup
1 (5-ounce) can evaporated milk
1 (8-ounce) jar pasteurized processed cheese spread

Cook broccoli for 5 minutes; drain. Transfer to casserole and mix in wild rice and next 4 ingredients. Refrigerate at least 8 hours or overnight. Cover with cheese spread. Bake at 350° for 35 minutes.
Yield: 6 to 8 servings

Ivy Coffey
Russell, IA

RICE PILAF

4 tablespoons butter
2 cups instant rice
2½ cups turkey broth or canned chicken broth
2 tablespoons dried onion flakes
Pinch of saffron
Pinch of salt
Pinch of pepper

Melt butter in large skillet. Add rice. Sauté, stirring constantly, until rice takes on color. Add broth and remaining ingredients. Mix thoroughly. Turn into 2-quart baking dish; cover. Bake at 425° for 20 to 25 minutes until liquid is absorbed and rice is tender.
Yield: 8 servings

Shirley Grenoble
Altoona, PA

TURKEY DUMPLINGS

2 cups all-purpose flour
1 teaspoon salt
4 teaspoons baking powder
3 tablespoons shortening, chilled
¾ cup milk
8 cups boiling turkey broth

Sift flour and next 2 ingredients. Cut in shortening with pastry blender until mixture resembles coarse meal. Mix in milk. Drop by teaspoonfuls into broth. Cover and simmer for 20 minutes.
Yield: 14 to 16 dumplings

Mike Halter
East Ridge, TN

SQUASH CASSEROLE

3 pounds yellow squash, cut into small pieces
1 medium onion, chopped
1 stick butter, melted
1 (8-ounce) package herb-seasoned stuffing mix, divided
½ (4-ounce) jar diced pimiento, drained
1 (10¾-ounce) can cream of chicken soup
1 (8-ounce) can sliced water chestnuts, drained
1 (8-ounce) carton sour cream
6 ounces shredded Cheddar cheese

Boil squash with onion until barely tender, about 5 minutes. Combine butter with the stuffing mix; transfer half to bottom of a casserole. Mix pimiento with next 3 ingredients, and add to squash. Place squash mixture in casserole. Sprinkle with cheese, and top with remaining stuffing mix. Bake at 350° for 30 minutes.
Yield: 8 to 10 servings

Laura Terrell
Sherman, TX

SUMMER SQUASH CASSEROLE

5 medium-size yellow squash, cut into 1-inch pieces
¼ pound pork sausage
1 small onion, chopped (optional)
1 (10¾-ounce) can cream of mushroom soup
½ soup can milk
½ (8-ounce) package shredded mild Cheddar cheese
1 cup breadcrumbs
1 egg, beaten

Boil squash until crisp-tender, about 7 to 10 minutes. Drain, and set aside. Brown sausage in skillet. Drain and crumble; then sauté onion in skillet until golden. Transfer squash, sausage-onion mixture, and remaining ingredients to 2-quart casserole. Bake at 350° for 30 minutes or brown and bubbling.
Yield: 4 to 6 servings

Allen Ricks
Morristown, TN

CONNOISSEUR'S CASSEROLE

1 (11-ounce) can white shoepeg corn, drained
1 (14½-ounce) can cut green beans
½ cup chopped celery
½ cup chopped onion
½ cup sour cream
½ cup grated sharp Cheddar cheese
1 (10¾-ounce) can cream of celery soup
½ teaspoon salt
½ teaspoon pepper
1 cup crushed round buttery crackers
½ stick butter, melted

Mix corn with next 8 ingredients. Transfer to a 2-quart casserole covered with nonstick cooking spray. Top with crackers; drizzle with butter. Bake at 350° for 45 minutes.
Yield: 8 servings

Marian West
Edgefield, SC

DEB'S CORN CASSEROLE

4 slices bacon, cooked, drained, and crumbled
2 (14¾-ounce) can cream-style corn
1 (15¼-ounce) can whole kernel corn, drained
1 (7-ounce) box cornbread mix
½ cup vegetable oil
2 teaspoons garlic powder
4 eggs, beaten
2 teaspoons crushed red pepper (optional)
1½ cups shredded sharp Cheddar cheese
Pinch of paprika

Into a 13x9x2-inch rectangular pan, combine bacon and next 7 ingredients. Top with cheese and sprinkle with paprika. Bake at 325°, uncovered, for 45 to 60 minutes until brown and bubbling.
Yield: 8 to 10 servings

Debbie Pleasants
Carbondale, IL

HOMINY CASSEROLE

1 stick butter, divided
¼ cup all-purpose flour
1 teaspoon onion powder
2 cups milk, heated
1 cup grated processed cheese loaf
2 (15½-ounce) cans hominy, drained
1 cup crushed round buttery crackers

Melt ½ stick butter over low heat. Blend in flour and onion powder. Slowly whisk in milk until thickened and smooth. Stir in cheese until melted. Add hominy. Pour into a greased, 2-quart casserole. Melt remaining butter; toss with crackers. Top casserole with buttered cracker crumbs. Bake at 350° for 30 minutes, or until hot and bubbling.
Yield: 6 servings

Susan Fowler
Tullahoma, TN

BAKED VIDALIA ONIONS

4 large Vidalia or other sweet onion
4 beef-flavored bouillon cubes, divided
4 tablespoons butter, divided
4 dashes Worcestershire sauce, divided
4 dashes Tabasco sauce, divided
4 pinches Greek seasoning or seasoned salt, divided

Peel onion. Cut a ½-inch slice from the top of each onion. With a spoon, scoop out 1 tablespoon onion from the top of each onion. In each onion, insert 1 bouillon cube, a tablespoon of butter, a dash of Worcestershire, a dash of Tabasco, and a pinch of Greek seasoning or seasoned salt. Double-wrap each onion in aluminum foil. Bake at 425° for 1 hour, or on a covered barbecue grill on medium-high heat for 1 hour.
Yield: 4 servings

Michael M. Tull
Roswell, GA

SHAKER ONION PIE

1 (9-inch) pie crust shell
1 egg white, beaten
2 medium onion, sliced thin
2 tablespoons butter
3 eggs, beaten
1½ cups sour cream
½ teaspoon salt
2 teaspoon caraway seed

Prick entire pie shell with fork. Beat egg white and brush, as needed, over pie shell. Bake shell in 200° oven for 10 minutes. Cool. Sauté onion in butter until golden, and let cool slightly. Add remaining ingredients to onion. Pour onion mixture onto pie shell. Bake on cookie sheet at 350° for 30 to 35 minutes, until center of pie is firm.
Yield: 8 servings

Diana Linder
Houston, TX

ASPARAGUS AND PEAS CASSEROLE

1 (8.5-ounce) can small, young peas, drained
½ (16-ounce) can pearl onions, drained
½ pound fresh asparagus, steamed
1 (10¾-ounce) can cream of mushroom soup
½ pound fresh mushrooms, sliced
¾ cup grated extra-sharp Cheddar cheese
½ (2.8-ounce) can fried onion rings

In 3-quart casserole, alternate layers of peas and the next 4 ingredients. Top with cheese. Bake at 350° for 45 minutes. Sprinkle onion rings on top, and bake an additional 10 minutes, or until lightly browned. *Serve with fried turkey.*
Yield: 4 servings

Michael M. Tull
Roswell, GA

SMOKED ROASTED ASPARAGUS IN GARLIC

2 tablespoons butter or margarine
4 cloves garlic, thinly sliced
2 tablespoons lemon juice
¼ teaspoon salt
¼ teaspoon pepper
1 small onion, thinly sliced
1½ pounds fresh asparagus, trimmed

Melt butter or margarine in small skillet over low heat. Add garlic and cook until tender. Remove from heat, and stir in lemon juice, salt, and pepper. Into 1-quart gratin dish, layer onion, then asparagus. Drizzle garlic mixture on top. Place dish in top cooking grate of smoker, uncovered. Cover smoker lid, and cook 1 hour or until asparagus is crisp-tender.
Yield: 6 servings

Masterbuilt Manufacturing Inc.
Columbus, GA

FRIED CABBAGE

3 slices bacon, chopped
½ medium onion, chopped
½ medium cabbage, chopped
1 ounce pimiento, sliced or chopped
Pinch of salt
Pinch of pepper
2 tablespoons sugar (optional)
3 to 4 tablespoons water

Fry bacon with the onion. Add cabbage and remaining ingredients.
Cover, and cook about 18 to 20 minutes, or until cabbage is tender.
Yield: 2 servings

Ed Andrews
Williamston, NC

WHITE SAUCE

2 tablespoons margarine, melted
2 tablespoons flour
¼ teaspoon salt
1 cup milk

Stir all ingredients until combined. Cook in microwave on High
power until thick, about 3½ minutes.
*Use for creamed peas, chipped beef, or add ½ cup processed cheese loaf to
make cheese sauce.*
Yield: about 1 cup

Ivy Coffey
Russell, IA

KETTLE GRAVY

¼ cup cold water or milk
2 tablespoons flour
1 cup hot turkey broth
Pinch of salt
Pinch of pepper

In covered jar, add water or milk, then flour. Shake until combined.
Stir flour-water mixture into broth and bring to a boil. Season with
salt and pepper.
Yield: about 1½ cups

Ivy Coffey
Russell, IA

PAN GRAVY

2 tablespoons turkey drippings or fat
2 tablespoons flour
1 cup milk
Salt, as needed
Pepper, as needed

Stir butter and flour together until smooth. Stir in milk slowly and cook over low heat until bubbly and thick. Season to taste.
Serve with fried turkey.
Yield: about 1¼ cups

Ivy Coffey
Russell, IA

SWEET AND HOT BEANS

1½ pounds bacon, fried, crumbled, 2 tablespoons grease reserved
2½ pounds onion, chopped
8 ounces brown sugar
1 teaspoon cayenne pepper
1 (114-ounce) can pork and beans

Cook onion in bacon grease; drain. Combine onion, bacon, brown sugar, and cayenne in a Dutch oven or bean pot. Stir well. Combine beans with other ingredients in pan. Mix well. Bake in oven at 350° for 1 hour.
Yield: 16 (4-ounce) servings

N.K. Farr, Jr.
Hattiesburg, MS

COLE SLAW

2½ cups finely shredded cabbage
1 teaspoon salt
1 cup mayonnaise
½ cup chopped cucumber
½ cup chopped green onions
1 teaspoon celery seed

Sprinkle cabbage with salt. Moisten with mayonnaise. Add cucumber and green onions. Sprinkle with celery seed.
Yield: 4 servings

Mary B. Miller
Amherst, OH

FAVORITE MARINATED SLAW

1 cup cider vinegar
1 cup sugar
1 teaspoon salt
1 cup water
1 teaspoon mustard seed
1½ quarts shredded cabbage
1 onion, chopped
1 bell pepper, chopped
1 (4-ounce) jar chopped pimientos, drained

Boil vinegar and next 4 ingredients. Cool slightly; then pour over remaining ingredients. Mix thoroughly. Refrigerate until cool.
Yield: 4 to 6 servings

James Earl and Mary Kennemer
Edgefield, SC

CORNBREAD DRESSING I

1 (8-ounce) package herb-seasoned stuffing mix
2 cups crumbled cornbread
½ cup melted butter or margarine
1 teaspoon bottled onion juice
1 cup diced onion
1 cup applesauce
1 (10¾-ounce) can cream of mushroom soup
1 teaspoon rubbed sage
1 teaspoon thyme
1 teaspoon marjoram
Pinch of salt
Pinch of pepper

Toss stuffing mix and cornbread with remaining ingredients. Add a little water to moisten dressing, if necessary. Place in a 13x9x2-inch pan and cook 30 minutes at 400°.
Yield: 8 to 10 servings

Ed Andrews
Williamston, NC

CORNBREAD DRESSING II

3 eggs, beaten
3 cups self-rising cornmeal
2 cups buttermilk
½ cup bacon drippings or vegetable oil
½ cup chopped celery
½ cup chopped onion
1 tablespoon rubbed sage
¼ teaspoon pepper
2 to 3 cups hot turkey broth

Mix eggs and next 3 ingredients. Pour into greased 12-inch ovenproof skillet. Bake at 350° for 20 minutes or until golden. Cool. Crumble cornbread into a large bowl. Add celery and next 3 ingredients. Stir in enough broth to moisten. Grease a 13x9x2-inch rectangular glass pan. Empty dressing into pan. Bake at 425° for 35 to 40 minutes, or until golden.
Yield: 10 to 12 servings

Bob Loyd
Memphis, TN

SOUTHERN-STYLE CORNBREAD DRESSING

4½ cups hot turkey stock
4 cups crumbled cornbread
4 eggs, lightly beaten
2 teaspoons salt
½ teaspoon pepper
1 cup chopped celery
1 cup chopped onion

Pour stock over cornbread. Add eggs and remaining ingredients. Mix thoroughly. Bake in 13x9x2-inch pan at 400° for 25 to 30 minutes.
Yield: 8 to 10 servings

Liz Szefcyk
Amherst, OH

CORNBREAD PECAN STUFFING

1 cup chopped celery
1 cup chopped bell pepper
1 cup chopped onion
1½ teaspoons poultry seasoning
2 teaspoons sage
1 stick margarine
1 tablespoon chicken-flavored bouillon granules or 3 cubes
2 cups boiling water
1 (16-ounce) package cornbread stuffing mix
1 cup chopped pecans, toasted
2 eggs, lightly beaten

Cook celery and next 4 ingredients in margarine until tender. In large bowl, dissolve bouillon in water. Add celery mixture, stuffing mix, pecans, and eggs, and mix well. Loosely stuff turkey just before roasting or bake in greased baking dish at 350° for 30 minutes or until heated.
Yield: 6 servings

Missouri Egg Merchandising Council
Columbia, MO

WALNUT POULTRY STUFFING

Giblets from 1 turkey
1 onion, sliced
1 bay leaf
1 cup water
½ pound stale bread, crusts removed, processed into crumbs
1 tablespoon salt
2 tablespoons poultry seasoning or sage
2 cups chopped walnuts
4 tablespoons butter, melted

Cook giblets, onion, and bay leaf in water until giblets are tender. Discard bay leaf. Finely chop giblets. Combine remaining ingredients. Moisten with giblet stock.
Yield: stuffing for a 12 to 14 pound turkey

Liz Szefcyk
Amherst, OH

FRUITED STUFFING

2 sticks margarine or butter
1 cup chopped onion
3 cups apples, cored, peeled, and diced
7 cups soft breadcrumbs
1 cup raisins
1½ teaspoons salt
½ teaspoon pepper
¼ teaspoon rubbed sage

Melt margarine or butter, and sauté onion and apples until tender.
Mix in breadcrumbs and remaining ingredients.
Yield: stuffing for a 12-pound turkey

Nancy Grayton
Rochester, NY

CHESTNUT STUFFING

1 pound chestnuts
2 large onions, diced
4 stalks celery, cubed
3 tablespoons vegetable oil
1 pound fresh mushrooms, sliced, or 1 (8-ounce) can sliced, liquid
   reserved
1 loaf whole-wheat bread, toasted and crumbled
2 eggs, slightly beaten
¾ teaspoon salt
½ teaspoon pepper
1 cup boiling water

Make a cross on each chestnut with a sharp knife. Boil chestnuts until
shell opens, about 10 minutes. Cool in cold water, peel, and dice. In a
large saucepan, sauté onion and celery in oil until opaque. Add fresh
mushrooms or canned mushrooms and liquid; cook 10 minutes
longer. Combine bread, chestnuts, and mushroom mixture with
remaining ingredients. Spoon into turkey; do not pack.
Yield: stuffing for a 12-pound turkey

GRANDMA DETTMER'S RAISIN STUFFING

1 medium onion, diced
2 heaping tablespoons shortening or 4 tablespoons vegetable oil
1½ loaves stale white bread
2 eggs, beaten
1½ cups raisins
1½ cups sugar
1 teaspoon salt
1 teaspoon pepper

In large skillet, sauté onion in shortening or oil until translucent. Moisten bread in water, several slices at a time. Squeeze out all moisture from bread; then tear into 1-inch pieces. Add bread to skillet and cook over medium heat until light brown. In a large bowl, mix the eggs and remaining ingredients. Stir egg mixture into the skillet; then stuff into turkey.
Yield: stuffing for 12-pound turkey

Robert Dettmer
Ironton, MO

OYSTER STUFFING

6 stalks celery, diced
1 teaspoon salt
1 medium onion, diced
2 sticks butter or margarine, divided
3 (8-ounce) bags herb-seasoned stuffing mix
2 pints oysters, drained and chopped

Put celery in a pan with water to cover. Add salt. Boil until tender. Sauté onion in 1 stick butter until clear. Drain celery, reserving liquid. Empty stuffing mix into a large bowl. Add the celery, onion, and oysters. Melt the remaining stick of butter. Slowly add enough celery water to moisten the stuffing. Stuff turkey or bake in casserole dish.
Yield: 8 to 10 servings

Sherry Haight
Mount Olive, MS

I started hunting as a young boy. Some of my best memories are of my dad and me hunting in the woods, and it is a sport that I still enjoy. It's woven into the very fabric of American culture, and it's to our credit that we have developed conservation programs that provide an abundance of wildlife resources to hunt and to watch. We have a great hunting heritage. Let's work together to keep it going.

John Anderson
Smithville, TN
Country Music Star

WHOLE WHEAT BREAD STUFFING

1 pound chestnuts
2 large onions, diced
4 stalks celery, cut into 1-inch slices
3 tablespoons oil
1 pound fresh mushrooms, sliced
1 (1-pound) loaf 100% whole wheat bread
2 eggs, slightly beaten
¾ teaspoon salt
½ teaspoon pepper
1 cup boiling water

Make a cross on each chestnut with sharp knife; boil until shell opens, about 10 minutes. Cool in cold water, peel, and slice; set aside. In a large saucepan, sauté onions and celery in oil until tender; add mushrooms and cook 10 minutes. Set aside. Toast bread slices until brown; cube and place in large bowl. Add chestnuts, onion mixture, eggs, salt, pepper, and boiling water. Mix well; stuff into turkey.
Yield: stuffing for a 16-pound turkey

WHITE MEAT, ANYONE?

Turkey Breast from Stuffed to Stir-Fried

Peter Reis © 1995

Natural resource conservation is a relatively new concept. The idea of "conservation through wise use" was made popular by Theodore Roosevelt in the early 1900s. Today wildlife conservation, aided by research and management programs, has been responsible for the restoration of many wildlife species that not too long ago were in danger of being eliminated, including the wild turkey.

John Lewis
Columbia, MO

GRILLED SPINACH-STUFFED TURKEY BREAST

1 cup stale bread, crusts removed, cubed
1 cup chopped celery, cut into ½-inch pieces
⅓ cup melted butter
¼ cup white wine or chicken broth
1 (10-ounce) package frozen chopped spinach, thawed and drained
6 slices bacon, fried crisp
1 medium onion, chopped
1 (5- to 7-pound) bone-in turkey breast
½ teaspoon salt
¼ teaspoon pepper
2 tablespoons butter, softened

Prepare grill for indirect cooking, and heat until coals turn into white ash. Make foil drip pan, and place opposite coals. In large bowl, stir together bread and next 6 ingredients. Fill stuffing in breast cavity. Close skin with toothpicks. (If any stuffing remains, heat in foil pan on grill during the last 30 minutes of cooking.) Season turkey with salt and pepper. Grill turkey breast for 2 to 2½ hours. Baste occasionally with softened butter.
Yield: 6 to 8 servings

FRIED WILD TURKEY BREAST

2 pounds wild turkey breast
1 pint buttermilk
1 cup flour
1 teaspoon salt
1 teaspoon pepper
Vegetable oil

Slice turkey breast into 1-inch strips. Marinate in buttermilk at least 8 hours, or overnight. Mix flour, salt, and pepper in a paper bag. Drop one turkey strip at a time in the bag, and shake each strip until battered. Deep fry in oil until golden.
Yield: 8 to 10 servings

Keith Foote
Toone, TN

CHICKEN FRIED WILD TURKEY BREAST

1 (5-pound) wild turkey breast, deboned and cut into strips
1 (16-ounce) bottle Italian dressing
2 eggs, beaten
2 cups milk
Salt, as needed
Pepper, as needed
2 cups flour
Shortening or oil, as needed

Marinate turkey strips in Italian dressing 8 hours or overnight. In small bowl, whisk eggs into milk. In second bowl, mix salt, pepper, and flour. Dip turkey strips in egg wash, then into batter. Deep fry in shortening or oil until golden. Drain on paper towels.
Serve with cream gravy made with 2 tablespoons flour combined in skillet with 2 tablespoons melted butter, salt, and pepper. Slowly add 1 cup mild; stir until thickened.
Yield: 8 to 10 servings

Lynda, Steve, and David Konarik
Houston, TX

FRIED TURKEY BREAST

1 (2-pound) boneless turkey breast, cut into ¼-inch slices
½ cup vegetable oil
½ cup dry vermouth
¾ teaspoon celery salt
1 teaspoon chervil
½ teaspoon lemon pepper
½ teaspoon savory
2 mushrooms, sliced

Place turkey slices in non-metal bowl. Add oil and next 5 ingredients, and mix well. Marinate turkey for 3 hours. Add 3 tablespoons marinade into large frying pan. Fry turkey slices quickly over high heat, about 2 minutes on each side, adding more marinade if necessary. Transfer meat to heated serving platter. Quickly sauté mushrooms in remaining marinade, and scatter atop turkey.
Serve over wild rice.
Yield: 4 servings

Harold Knight
Cadiz, KY

DELORIS'
CHICKEN FRIED TURKEY

2 cups flour
1 tablespoon Greek seasoning
Salt to taste
Pepper to taste
2 teaspoons garlic powder
2 pounds turkey breast strips
Vegetable oil

Mix flour and next 4 ingredients. Roll strips in flour mixture. Fry in shallow skillet on medium heat in oil until turkey is browned on both sides. Cover, and cook 3 to 4 minutes until turkey is tender and cooked through.
Save grease drippings for milk gravy.
Yield: 4 to 6 servings

Deloris Blount Hook
Wynne, AR

FRIED TURKEY FINGERS

2 eggs, slightly beaten
1 cup milk
3 cups self-rising flour
⅓ cup lemon pepper
1 teaspoon cayenne pepper
½ (5-pound) wild turkey breast, deboned, cut into thin strips
3 to 4 cups peanut oil

Mix eggs and milk in a bowl. In a paper bag, combine flour and next 2 ingredients. Dip turkey fingers into the egg batter, then drop fingers, 6 to 8 at a time, into bag with flour mixture. Shake. Fry fingers in oil for about 3 minutes, or until golden.
Yield: 4 to 6 servings

Paul Ferrell
Hattiesburg, MS

PRIMOS
FRIED TURKEY STRIPS

1 cup flour
⅓ cup yellow cornmeal
Salt, pepper, garlic powder, or cayenne pepper to taste
1 cup milk
1 (5-pound) uncooked turkey breast
Vegetable oil

Combine the flour and cornmeal. Add seasonings to taste; set aside. Skin the turkey, remove the meat from the bone, and slice the uncooked meat into 1½-inch strips. Dip turkey strips into milk then into batter; place in hot oil (at least 1½ inches in skillet). Fry until tender; then drain on paper towels.
Yield: 6 servings

Will Primos
Primos Hunting Calls and Accessories
Jackson, MS

JERRY'S FAVORITE FRIED WILD TURKEY

2 cups buttermilk
½ teaspoon pepper
½ teaspoon seasoned salt
Pinch of poultry seasoning
1 (5-pound) whole wild turkey breast, deboned and cut into ½-inch
   slices
3 cups self-rising flour
1 quart peanut oil

Combine buttermilk and next 3 ingredients. Into a covered bowl, layer turkey then cover with buttermilk mixture; continue layering and end with buttermilk mixture. Cover tightly, and refrigerate 12 hours or overnight. Dredge turkey slices in flour and deep fry until golden.
Yield: 6 to 8 servings

Kris Gardner
Harpersville, AL

UNBELIEVABLE CAJUN TURKEY BREAST

2 eggs
2 tablespoons water
1 (3- to 4-pound) wild turkey breast, deboned, cut into strips or
   nuggets
1 (16-ounce) package Mo's Mix Cajun Recipe Season-All Coating Mix
Nonstick cooking spray or vegetable oil

Beat eggs and water. Roll turkey in egg wash, then coat generously with Cajun mix. Bake at 375° on nonstick baking sheet 30 to 40 minutes, or pan fry in ½ inch of oil, or deep fry until done.
Yield: 6 to 8 servings

Mo Skaggs
Rolla, MO

TURKEY BREAST MEDALLIONS WITH PECAN HONEY GLAZE

1 (1½-pound) boneless turkey breast
Salt, as desired
Pepper, as desired
2 cups all-purpose flour
6 eggs
⅔ cup milk
Vegetable oil, as needed

GLAZE

1¼ cups honey
1¼ cups roasted pecans, finely chopped

Slice the turkey breast into 12, 2-ounce medallions. Combine salt, pepper, and flour. Beat eggs and milk together. Heat ½-inch oil in a skillet. Dredge turkey in flour mixture, dip into egg mixture, and again in flour. Fry turkey on one side until golden. Turn, and brown other side until completely cooked. Drain turkey on paper towels. Heat honey; stir in the pecans. Place turkey on a platter and top with honey-pecan mixture. Serve immediately.
Yield: 4 servings

Kirk Williams, CCE
Sacramento, CA

HOT AND WILD
TURKEY STRIPS

1 (2-pound) boneless wild turkey breast
2 eggs, beaten
2 teaspoons lemon pepper
Salt to taste
Pepper to taste
1 teaspoon to 2 tablespoons Tabasco sauce
Flour, as needed
Shortening, as needed

Pound turkey breast to tenderize. Then cut into strips. Mix eggs and next 4 ingredients. Soak turkey in egg mixture for 5 minutes. Dip strips in flour. Deep fry until golden.
Yield: 4 servings

Jerry Bryant
Excelsior Springs, MO

SWISS TURKEY BREAST
OVER RICE

2 large boneless turkey breasts, cut into 3 portions each
Nonstick cooking spray
6 slices Swiss cheese
1 (10¾-ounce) can cream of mushroom soup
¼ cup milk
1 (8-ounce) bag herb-seasoned stuffing mix
½ stick butter or margarine, melted

Arrange turkey breasts in a lightly-greased, 3-quart baking dish. Top with cheese. Combine soup and milk in bowl. Spoon over cheese. Sprinkle with stuffing mix. Drizzle butter on top. Cover, and bake at 350° for 1 hour.
Serve over wild rice.
Yield: 6 servings

Tom and Kathy Karsten
Allendale, MI

BEAN RIDGE BAKED TURKEY

4 ounces shredded dried beef
1 (2-pound) boneless turkey breast, cut into 8 pieces
8 slices bacon
1 (10¾-ounce) cream of mushroom soup
1 (16-ounce) carton sour cream

Cover bottom of a greased casserole with beef. Wrap each turkey piece with a bacon slice. Secure with a toothpick. Set turkey pieces on beef. Combine soup and sour cream, and spoon on top of turkey. Bake at 275°, uncovered, for 1½ to 2 hours.
Yield: 4 to 6 servings

Prosser Family
Alexander County, IL

TURKEY CASSEROLE

6 cups chopped cooked turkey breast
1 (12-ounce) package frozen broccoli cuts, thawed
1 (10¾-ounce) can cream of mushroom soup
1 cup mayonnaise
Pinch of salt
2 cups shredded mozzarella cheese

Put turkey in baking dish. Top with broccoli. Combine soup with mayonnaise and salt, and pour over vegetables. Cover with cheese. Bake at 350° for 25 to 30 minutes.
Yield: 6 servings

Mary Harris
Makanda, IL

BAKED TURKEY TENDERLOINS IN BARBECUE SAUCE

2 (8-ounce) boneless turkey breast tenderloins, halved
2 tablespoons water
¼ cup cider vinegar
¼ cup ketchup
½ teaspoon dry mustard
½ teaspoon Worcestershire sauce
3 tablespoons minced onion
1 clove garlic, minced or pressed
1 drop Tabasco sauce
Salt to taste
Pepper to taste

Arrange turkey pieces in a baking dish. Combine water and remaining ingredients, and mix well. Spoon over turkey. Bake, uncovered, at 350° for 15 to 20 minutes, or until turkey is no longer pink in thickest part. Baste once or twice.
Yield: 4 servings

Iowa Turkey Federation
Ames, IA

TURKEY KIEV

½ cup breadcrumbs
¼ teaspoon salt
2 teaspoons Parmesan cheese
1 teaspoon basil
1 teaspoon oregano
1 (3-pound) uncooked boneless turkey breast, cut into 2-inch cubes
½ stick butter, melted

SAUCE

¼ cup apple juice
¼ cup minced onion
¼ cup chopped parsley

Mix breadcrumbs and next 4 ingredients. Dip turkey in melted butter, then in crumb topping. Bake at 375° for 30 minutes. Combine apple juice, onion, parsley, and any remaining butter. Pour sauce over turkey. Bake 5 minutes longer.
Yield: 4 to 6 servings

Susie Brown
Edgefield, SC

SHANGHAI TURKEY CUTLETS

2 tablespoons flour
½ teaspoon paprika
¼ teaspoon pepper
1 pound turkey cutlets
1 cup sliced mushrooms
½ cup dry sherry
2 tablespoons brown sugar
⅓ cup water
1 tablespoon reduced-sodium soy sauce
1 tablespoon sesame seeds
1 teaspoon ground ginger

Combine flour, paprika, and pepper. Dredge cutlets in flour mixture. Coat skillet with nonstick cooking spray. Brown cutlets on both sides, about 5 minutes. Remove, and arrange on shallow baking dish. Sauté mushrooms in skillet, about 5 minutes. Top cutlets with mushrooms. Add sherry and remaining ingredients to skillet, and bring to a boil. Pour over cutlets. Cover tightly, and bake at 300° for 20 to 25 minutes, or until cutlets have an internal temperature of 160°.
Yield: 4 servings

Iowa Turkey Federation
Ames, IA

SHAKE 'N' FRY TURKEY

2 cups milk
3 eggs, beaten
8 ounces breadcrumbs
8 wild turkey breast fillets (¼ inch thick, 3 inches long, 1½ inches wide)
Vegetable oil

In a medium bowl, mix milk and eggs. Place breadcrumbs in another bowl. Immerse turkey breasts in milk mixture, then in breadcrumbs; repeat process for double breading (which seals out excess grease from meat). Heat about 2 inches of oil in iron skillet. Drop turkey into oil for about 10 minutes, turning once. Remove turkey and drain on paper towels. Serve with Running Gear Gravy made from the neck, back, giblets, legs, and thighs, which are cooked, browned, seasoned, cut up, and added to thickened turkey broth.
Yield: 6 to 8 servings

Rob Keck
Edgefield, SC

DILLED BARBECUED TURKEY BREAST

1 cup plain yogurt
¼ cup minced parsley
¼ cup chopped green onions
3 tablespoons vegetable oil
2 tablespoons lemon juice
2 tablespoons chopped dill
1 clove garlic, minced
½ teaspoon dried rosemary
½ teaspoon salt
½ teaspoon pepper
1 (2- to 3-pound) bone-in turkey breast half
Nonstick cooking spray

Prepare grill for indirect cooking. In small bowl, combine yogurt and next 9 ingredients. Place turkey in 13x9x2-inch rectangular pan, and pierce skin several times with a fork. Spread yogurt mixture evenly over breast. Cover, and refrigerate 6 hours or overnight. Coat grill with nonstick vegetable spray. Place turkey breast on grill, cover, and cook 1½ hours, or until meat thermometer, inserted into thickest portion, registers 170° to 175°, or until juices run clear.
Yield: 5 to 6 servings

Berniece Greene
4th Place, National Turkey Federation recipe contest

GRILLED TURKEY BREAST

1 (5- to 6-pound) turkey breast
5 to 6 cups hickory chips, soaked in water at least 30 minutes
Nonstick cooking spray

Prepare covered grill for indirect heat. Scatter hickory chips over hot coals. Spray grill rack with nonstick cooking spray, and place over coals. Place turkey breast on rack, and grill for 1 to 1½ hours or until meat thermometer, inserted in thickest portion away from bone, registers 170° to 175°. Remove breast from grill and cool for 1 hour in refrigerator. Remove and discard skin. Slice before serving.
Yield: 6 to 8 servings

Terry Steele
Homosassa, FL

GRILLED TERIYAKI
WILD TURKEY BREAST

1 (4-pound) wild turkey breast half, deboned
1 large, heavy-duty, zip-top plastic bag
1 (8-ounce) bottle teriyaki sauce
1 (20-ounce) can pineapple slices
1 teaspoon pepper
1 teaspoon garlic salt

Place turkey breast in plastic bag, add entire bottle of teriyaki sauce and juice from pineapples. Marinate in refrigerator at least 8 hours, or overnight. Remove turkey from bag, sprinkle with pepper and garlic salt, and grill on both sides until done. Serve with pineapple slices.
Be careful not to overcook. Slice meat across the grain.
Serve with wild rice and stir-fried vegetables.
Yield: 4 servings

Nell Davis
Ridgeland, SC

TURKEY KEBABS

½ (5-pound) wild turkey breast, deboned and cut into 1-inch cubes
Soy sauce, as needed
Teriyaki sauce, as needed
1 teaspoon garlic salt
1 red bell pepper, cubed
1 small zucchini, cubed
1 onion, sliced
1 pound fresh mushrooms

Place turkey cubes in large bowl. Cover with half soy sauce and half teriyaki sauce. Add garlic salt, and mix thoroughly. Marinate in refrigerator 8 hours, or overnight. Drain turkey pieces, reserving marinade. Alternate pieces of turkey, bell pepper, zucchini, onion, and mushroom on skewers. Grill over charcoal fire or broil in the oven. Baste with marinade if desired.
Yield: 4 to 6 servings

Rebecca Nix
Mount Vernon, IL

DAD'S FAVORITE TURKEY KEBABS

3 ears corn, cut into 1-inch pieces
3 medium zucchinis, cut into ¾-inch pieces
2 red bell peppers, cut into 1-inch cubes
2 (8-ounce) turkey tenderloins, cut into 1-inch cubes
⅓ cup low-calorie Italian dressing, divided

In medium saucepan over high heat, parboil corn, about 1 to 2 minutes. Remove corn, and plunge into cold water. In large glass bowl, add corn, zucchini, red pepper, turkey, and ¼ cup dressing. Cover, and refrigerate 2 hours. Drain turkey and vegetables; discard marinade. Alternately thread turkey cubes and vegetables ½-inch apart on skewers. Grill kebabs 18 to 20 minutes, brushing with remaining dressing, turning skewers after first 10 minutes.
Yield: 4 servings

Iowa Turkey Federation
Ames, IA

TURKEY FAJITAS

1 pound boneless turkey breast
4 slices red onion, cut ¼ inch thick
2 tablespoons olive oil
2 tablespoons lime juice
2 large bell peppers, halved
2 cloves garlic, minced
¾ cup salsa
8 (7-inch) flour tortillas, warmed
1 cup shredded mild Cheddar cheese

Combine turkey and next 6 ingredients in a large, heavy-duty zip-top plastic bag. Seal; then marinate 2 to 24 hours in the refrigerator. Grill or broil turkey, onion, and peppers 4 to 5 inches from heat, for 5 to 8 minutes per side while boiling marinade. Cut turkey and vegetables into thin strips, and divide among tortillas. Drizzle with hot marinade. Sprinkle with cheese. Roll up, and serve immediately.
Yield: 4 servings

Mary Jo Burke
Westby, WI

TURKEY ENCHILADAS

1 (2-pound) boneless turkey breast
½ cup water
3 cloves garlic, divided
1 onion, chopped
3 tablespoons margarine
2 (4½-ounce) cans green chiles
1 tablespoon chili powder
½ teaspoon cumin
½ teaspoon salt
¼ teaspoon oregano
2 tablespoons cornstarch
1 cup chicken broth
1 cup evaporated skim milk
12 corn tortillas
1½ cups shredded Monterey Jack cheese, divided
6 green onions

Place turkey, water, and 1 clove garlic into saucepan. Simmer 15 minutes, reserving broth. Cut turkey into strips. Sauté onion in margarine. Add chiles and next 5 ingredients. Cook 1 minute. Stir in reserved and canned broth and milk. Heat until thickened; then remove from heat and stir in 1 cup cheese. Mix 1 cup cheese sauce with turkey. Divide turkey and sauce among tortillas. Fold tortillas, and place seam side down in baking dish. Cover with remaining cheese sauce. and sprinkle with green onions and remaining cheese. Bake at 400° for 20 minutes.
Yield: 6 servings

Mary Jo Burke
Westby, WI

91

MEXICAN TURKEY

2 (2-pound) boneless turkey breasts, cut into 1-inch pieces
Salt to taste
Cayenne pepper to taste
¼ cup bacon drippings
¼ cup almonds, blanched
⅓ cup seedless raisins
1½ cups pineapple chunks, drained
⅛ teaspoon ground cloves
⅛ teaspoon cinnamon
1½ cups orange juice
2 tablespoons flour
¼ cup water

Season turkey with salt and cayenne pepper. Cover with bacon drippings; set aside. In a Dutch oven, combine almonds and next 5 ingredients. Simmer, covered, for 10 minutes; then add turkey. Stir gently and cut back heat. Cook for 50 minutes longer. Thicken sauce with paste of flour and water before serving.
Yield: 8 to 10 servings

Shirley Grenoble
Altoona, PA

TURKEY YAKITORI

½ teaspoon low-sodium chicken bouillon granules
2 tablespoons boiling water
2 tablespoons low-sodium soy sauce
2 tablespoons dry sherry or white wine
1 teaspoon ginger
1 clove garlic, pressed
1 (1-pound) boneless turkey breast, cut into 1-inch cubes
3 green onions, cut into 2-inch lengths
¾ cup chopped bell pepper

Dissolve bouillon in water. Mix in soy sauce and next 3 ingredients. Transfer to zip-top plastic bag, add turkey, and seal. Marinate in refrigerator at least 4 hours. Thread turkey onto skewers with green onions and bell pepper. Grill over coals or broil 6 inches from heat, 4 to 5 minutes on each side. While cooking, baste with remaining marinade.
Yield: 2 servings

Iowa Turkey Federation
Ames, IA

TURKEY TENDERLOIN

½ **cup soy sauce**
2 **tablespoons vegetable oil**
2 **tablespoons dried onion flakes**
2 **tablespoons fresh lemon juice**
½ **cup sherry or other wine**
½ **teaspoon ground ginger**
Pinch of garlic powder
Pinch of salt
Pinch of pepper
1 **pound turkey breast tenderloin**

Combine soy sauce and next 8 ingredients. Marinate turkey breast in soy mixture at least 4 hours or overnight, turning frequently. Grill turkey over hot coals for 6 to 8 minutes on each side, until meat is no longer pink inside.
Yield: 2 servings

Iowa Turkey Federation
Ames, IA

ASIAN TURKEY STIR-FRY

1 **pound turkey breast slices**
2 **tablespoons vegetable oil**
1 **pound bok choy, sliced**
1 **(8-ounce) can sliced water chestnuts, drained**
1 **cup sliced fresh mushrooms**
3 **green onions, sliced**

SAUCE

1 **cup chicken broth**
¼ **cup soy sauce**
2 **tablespoons dry sherry**
2 **tablespoons cornstarch**
¼ **teaspoon garlic powder**
¼ **teaspoon ground ginger**

Cut turkey into thin strips. Heat oil in wok or skillet on medium-high heat, about 2 to 3 minutes. Add turkey. Stir-fry about 5 minutes. Remove turkey. Drain. Combine sauce ingredients; set aside. Add bok choy and next 3 ingredients to wok. Stir-fry 5 minutes. Pour sauce over vegetables. Return turkey to wok. Heat 2 to 3 minutes more, stirring until sauce thickens.
Serve over rice or chow mein noodles.
Yield: 4 servings

Missouri Poultry Federation
Columbia, MO

STIR-FRIED TURKEY BREAST

1 envelope Lipton Recipe Secrets Savory Herb and Garlic Soup Mix
1 cup water
1 pound boneless wild turkey breast, cut into thin strips
1 (10-ounce) package frozen mixed vegetables

In large skillet, combine soup mix and water; boil, stirring occasionally, for 5 to 10 minutes, until slightly thickened. Add turkey to skillet. Cook, uncovered, stirring frequently, about 5 to 10 minutes more, until turkey is done. Add vegetables. Cover, and simmer until vegetables are done.
Serve over fettuccine or rice.
Yield: 4 servings

Teresa Simons
Hallsville, MO

GARLIC-ROSEMARY TURKEY STIR FRY

1 (1-pound) boneless turkey breast, cut into bite-size strips
1 tablespoon olive oil
1 garlic clove, minced
2 teaspoons fresh rosemary
3 cups chopped fresh vegetables, such as broccoli, cauliflower,
**   zucchini, yellow squash, green onions, asparagus, green beans,**
**   wax beans, and cabbage**
¾ cup chicken broth
Hot cooked rice
½ cup cashews

In a large skillet or wok, stir-fry half the turkey in olive oil for about 2 minutes, or until turkey is cooked. Repeat with remaining turkey. Remove turkey from pan and keep warm. In the same pan over medium heat, cook garlic and rosemary until fragrant, about 1 minute. Stir in vegetables and broth. Bring to a boil; then reduce heat. Cover, and cook the mixture for 3 minutes. Return turkey to the pan. Toss to coat and heat through. Serve over rice. Sprinkle with cashews.
Yield: 4 to 6 servings

Mary Jo Burke
Westby, WI

WILD TURKEY STIR-FRY

¼ cup orange juice
1½ tablespoons cornstarch
1 (1-pound) boneless, skinless turkey breast, cut into strips
¾ cup chicken broth
1½ tablespoons soy sauce
2½ tablespoons vegetable oil
1 clove garlic, minced
1½ teaspoons ground ginger
1 cup chopped broccoli
1½ cup snow peas or green beans
1 medium red bell pepper, cut into thin strips
¾ cup sliced green onions
1 medium carrot, cut into thin slices
2 cups cooked white or wild rice

In a shallow glass bowl, combine orange juice and cornstarch. Add turkey, and stir to combine. Cover, and chill for 2 hours. Drain turkey, and discard juice mixture. Combine chicken broth and soy sauce. Set aside. In a wok or large skillet on medium heat, add oil, garlic, and ginger. Stir-fry for 30 seconds. Add broccoli and next 4 ingredients, and stir-fry until crisp-tender, about 5 minutes. Stir in broth mixture. Simmer about 1 minute. Serve over rice.
Yield: 4 servings

Dolores Renfrow
Morgantown, KY

PEAR AND APPLE STIR-FRY

1 pound turkey cutlets or slices, cut into ¼-inch strips
3 teaspoons vegetable oil, divided
1 teaspoon minced fresh ginger
¼ teaspoon salt
¼ teaspoon pepper
1 pear, cored and peeled, cut into ¼-inch strips
1 Rome Beauty or cooking apple, cored and peeled, and cut into ¼-inch strips
1 tablespoon lemon juice
1 tablespoon raspberry vinegar
½ cup halved green grapes

In medium bowl, combine turkey, 1 teaspoon oil, and next 3 ingredients. Cover and refrigerate. In another medium bowl, combine pear and apple with lemon juice and vinegar. Stir-fry fruit in 1 teaspoon oil for 1 minute. Remove fruit to a platter, and keep warm. In a skillet, heat 1 teaspoon oil over medium-high heat. Add turkey and stir-fry for 2½ to 3 minutes, or until turkey is no longer pink in center. Gently fold fruit and grapes into skillet, and heat until warm throughout.
Yield: 4 servings

Iowa Turkey Federation
Ames, IA

GARDEN-FRESH TURKEY STIR-FRY

1 (8-ounce) boneless turkey breast, cut into ¼-inch strips
¼ teaspoon pepper
¼ teaspoon salt
¼ teaspoon garlic powder
¼ teaspoon paprika
4 teaspoons margarine, divided
¾ cup thinly sliced yellow squash
1 cup cubed bell pepper
½ cup snow peas
¼ teaspoon Italian seasoning
4 to 5 cherry tomatoes

In a zip-top plastic bag, combine turkey and next 4 ingredients. In a wok or large skillet, heat 3 teaspoons margarine over medium-high heat. Add turkey, and stir-fry 2 to 3 minutes, or until meat is no longer pink. Remove from pan. Add remaining margarine, squash, bell pepper, and snow peas. Cook 1 minute. Sprinkle with Italian seasoning. Stir-fry until vegetables are crisp-tender. Stir in turkey and cherry tomatoes. Heat until warm.
Yield: 2 servings

Iowa Turkey Federation
Ames, IA

WILD TURKEY MEDALLIONS IN HERB SAUCE

2 (2-pound) boneless wild turkey breasts, partially thawed
Flour, as needed
Salt, as needed
Pepper, as needed
2 tablespoons butter
2 tablespoons olive oil

HERB SAUCE

¼ cup chopped cilantro leaves
¼ cup chopped capers, drained
2 tablespoons minced onion
2 tablespoons fresh lemon juice
2 garlic cloves, minced
1 teaspoon Dijon mustard
½ cup olive oil

Slice turkey across the grain into thin medallions. When breasts have defrosted completely, dredge in flour, and sprinkle with salt and pepper. Heat butter and olive oil in skillet, and sauté breasts on both sides, until golden. For herb sauce, combine cilantro and next 5 ingredients. Vigorously whisk in olive oil until well blended. Let sauce stand for 1 hour at room temperature before serving. Serve sauce with turkey.
Yield: 8 servings

Diana Linder
Houston, TX

JOY BENNETT'S SPECIALTY TURKEY BREASTS

1 (2-pound) boneless turkey breast
Pinch of salt
Pinch of pepper
Flour, as needed
2 tablespoons vegetable oil
3 (6-ounce) cans mushroom sauce
1 (0.6-ounce) package au jus mix
1½ cups water
3 (4-ounce) cans whole or sliced mushrooms, drained

Season turkey breast with salt and pepper. Dust in flour. Brown meat in oil on both sides in a pan that can be placed in oven. Add mushroom sauce, and remaining ingredients. Sprinkle enough flour to thicken gravy, but do not stir. Bring to a boil, and reduce heat to simmer. Place pan in a 350° oven for 45 minutes; cook until tender.
Yield: 4 to 6 servings

Joy Bennett
Buffalo, MO

CAJUN MARDI GRAS WILD TURKEY BREAST

1 pound bacon, diced into ¼ inches
Cajun poultry seasoning, as needed
4 tablespoons butter or margarine, divided
1½ cups chopped onion
1 (2-pound) boneless turkey breast, cut into 1-inch chunks
4 tablespoons vegetable oil, divided
1 tablespoon Worcestershire sauce

In a large heavy skillet, add bacon, sprinkle with 1 tablespoon Cajun seasoning; fry until crisp. Drain, discard grease, and set aside. In same skillet, add 1 tablespoon butter and sauté onion until tender. Remove onion and set aside. In a large bowl, combine turkey, 2 tablespoons oil, Worcestershire sauce, and remaining Cajun seasoning. To same skillet, heat remaining butter and oil until sizzling. Add turkey, bacon, and onion. Sauté until turkey is brown and tender.
Serve over rice.
Yield: 4 to 6 servings

Dave Constantine
Durand, WI

TURKEY CHASSEUR

2 (2-pound) turkey breasts, deboned and halved
Flour, as needed
Pinch of salt
Pinch of pepper
1 stick butter or margarine
½ pound mushrooms, sliced
3 ounces dry vermouth or dry white wine
⅛ teaspoon dried thyme
1 small bay leaf
1 (14½-ounce) can chicken broth

Dust turkey breasts with flour. Season with salt and pepper. Melt butter in large skillet over medium heat, and brown on all sides. Add mushrooms, and when lightly browned, add vermouth and remaining ingredients. Cover, and simmer 30 minutes, or until meat is tender. Transfer turkey breasts to a platter. Make gravy from pan juices and mushrooms. Pour over turkey and serve.
Yield: 8 to 10 servings

Doug and Mary Chester
Central Pennsylvania

WILD TURKEY DELIGHT

4 tablespoons butter
1 (5-pound) wild turkey breast, deboned, cut into 1-inch cubes
½ cup Wild Turkey bourbon
1 cup chicken broth
1 tablespoon cornstarch
1 tablespoon water
½ teaspoon salt
¼ teaspoon pepper
1 cup sour cream

Melt butter in skillet. Brown turkey cubes. Pour bourbon over turkey, and cook for 5 minutes or until bourbon evaporates. Add chicken broth, cover, and simmer 50 minutes, or until turkey is tender. Remove turkey and keep warm. In small bowl, mix cornstarch and water; stir into pan drippings. Cook until mixture thickens. Add salt, pepper, and sour cream, and heat until gravy simmers. Pour gravy over turkey.
Serve with noodles or rice.
Yield: 10 to 12 servings

Jerry Zimmerman
Alburtis, PA

MICROWAVED TURKEY BREAST WITH SAGE STUFFING

2 tablespoons butter
1 cup finely chopped onion
½ cup chopped celery
6 slices day-old bread, cubed (about 4 cups)
½ teaspoon poultry seasoning
½ teaspoon rubbed sage
1 tablespoon chopped parsley
1 pound turkey breast slices, cut ¼ inch thick
½ teaspoon salt
½ teaspoon pepper
½ cup chicken broth

Put butter and next 2 ingredients in an 8-inch-square microwave-safe dish. Cover with lid or vented plastic wrap, and microwave on High for 3 to 4 minutes, until tender. Stir in bread and next 3 ingredients. Empty bread mixture dish into a bowl. Place turkey on bottom of microwave dish in a single layer. Sprinkle with salt and pepper. Spoon bread mixture over turkey; add chicken broth. Cover, and microwave on High for 4 to 6 minutes, until center of turkey is barely pink when inserted with a knife tip. Let stand, uncovered, for 2 to 3 minutes until cooked thoroughly.
Yield: 4 servings

Missouri Poultry Federation
Columbia, MO

TUSCAN TURKEY CHEESE STEAK SANDWICHES

½ cup sundried tomatoes packed in oil, drained
¼ cup reduced-calorie mayonnaise
1 teaspoon lemon zest
½ teaspoon ground cumin
¼ teaspoon cayenne pepper
1½ cups sliced red bell pepper
1½ cups slice onion
¼ cup olive oil, divided
1 pound cooked turkey breast, cut into 4 (½-inch) slices
4 English muffins, split and lightly toasted
1 cup shredded mozzarella cheese

In small bowl, combine tomatoes and next 4 ingredients. Cover, and refrigerate until ready to use. In large skillet over medium heat, sauté bell pepper and onion in 2 teaspoons oil for 5 to 6 minutes, until vegetables are crisp-tender; remove vegetables from skillet. Add remaining oil to skillet; sauté turkey for 3 to 5 minutes, or until turkey is lightly browned on both sides. Spread tomato mixture over bottom half of each muffin, and top with one turkey slice and ¼ of the vegetable mixture. Top with mozzarella cheese, and broil 1 to 2 minutes or until cheese is melted. Top each with other muffin half.
Yield: 4 servings

Priscilla Yee
3rd Place, National Turkey Federation recipe contest

THAI TURKEY TOSS

1 pound turkey breast cutlets
1 cup water, lightly salted
5 ounces rice vermicelli or angel hair pasta
3 cups boiling water
2 cups shredded fresh spinach
1½ cups Granny Smith apples, cored and diced
½ cup grated carrot
½ cup peeled and diced zucchini
⅓ cup coarsely chopped dry-roasted peanuts
2 tablespoons chopped fresh basil

DRESSING

¼ cup fish sauce or soy sauce
3 tablespoons fresh lime juice
2 tablespoons brown sugar
1½ teaspoons minced fresh ginger
1 large clove garlic, minced
¼ teaspoon dried red pepper flakes

In large skillet, arrange turkey in a single layer. Add water, and bring
to a boil; cover. Reduce heat, and simmer 5 to 10 minutes, or until
turkey is no longer pink inside. Allow turkey to cool; then cut into
1½x¼-inch strips. Break vermicelli into 3-inch pieces and place in
bowl with boiling water. Allow pasta to stand 6 to 8 minutes, or until
soft; drain well. In large bowl, combine turkey, vermicelli, spinach,
and next 5 ingredients. To make dressing, combine fish sauce with
remaining ingredients. To serve, toss turkey mixture with dressing,
and divide evenly on four plates.
Rice vermicelli and fish sauce are available in Asian markets.
Yield: 4 servings

Judy Warren
1st Place, National Turkey Federation recipe contest

103

CANTALOUPE TURKEY SALAD DELIGHT

¾ pound, fully cooked smoked turkey breast, cut into ¼-inch cubes
¾ pound cantaloupe, cut into cubes or balls
1 cup chopped celery
½ cup thinly sliced green onions
1 tablespoon olive oil
1 tablespoon white wine vinegar
1½ teaspoons sesame oil
1½ teaspoons Dijon mustard
1½ teaspoons reduced-sodium soy sauce
⅛ teaspoon red pepper flakes
1 large garlic clove, minced

In large bowl, combine turkey and next 3 ingredients. In small bowl, whisk oil with next 6 ingredients; then combine mixtures. Cover, and refrigerate 1 hour.
Yield: 6 servings

Iowa Turkey Federation
Ames, IA

MARINATED WILD TURKEY ROLLS

1 (5-pound) wild turkey breast, deboned
12 ounces commercial Italian dressing
12 strips thickly sliced bacon

Cut breast meat along the grain into long, thin ¼-inch-thick strips. Submerge strips in dressing, cover, and marinate in the refrigerator for 3 to 6 hours. Drain. Wrap each meat strip in bacon, roll into a pinwheel, and secure with a toothpick. Place in a large nonstick skillet, and cook over very low heat for about an hour.
The turkey roll is done before bacon browns.
Yield: 6 servings

Gary L. Crafton
Coffeeville, MS

HAWAIIAN TURKEY BREAST

1 (8-ounce) bottle teriyaki sauce
1 (8-ounce) can crushed pineapple
¼ teaspoon ginger
1 (3-pound) boneless turkey breast

Combine teriyaki sauce and next 2 ingredients. Pour over turkey breast. Cover and marinate at least 8 hours, or overnight. Grill over a mesquite charcoal fire for approximately 20 minutes per side.
Yield: 6 servings

Boyd Burrow
Pearl, MS

INDONESIAN FIRE-ROASTED TURKEY

4 cloves garlic
⅔ cup peanut butter
3 green onions, chopped
1 small onion, quartered
2 tablespoons cilantro
1 tablespoon chopped ginger
⅓ cup dry sherry
⅓ cup soy sauce
2 tablespoons rice vinegar
¼ teaspoon red pepper flakes
1 (5- to 6-pound) whole turkey breast, halved

In blender or food processor, purée garlic and next 9 ingredients until smooth. Place turkey breasts in glass bowl. Coat well on both sides. Marinate 6 hours, or overnight. Heat gas grill 10 minutes on High. Reduce heat to Medium for cooking. Grill turkey breasts, bone side down. Use indirect heat; cook 1½ hours or until meat thermometer inserted in deepest portion of breast, registers 170° to 175°, and juices run clear. Maintain grill temperature at 350°.
To serve, slice breast meat and serve warm.
Yield: 8 servings

Molly A. Hosner
Honorable mention, National Turkey Federation recipe contest

A cousin introduced me to the wild turkey, and a friend is responsible for my involvement in the National Wild Turkey Federation. I am eternally grateful to both of them. The NWTF is a vital part of my life and that of each member of my family. We're proud of the NWTF's accomplishments and truly thankful we are a small part of the greatest of all conservation organizations whose focus is God, country, family, and the wild turkey. The memories and close personal friendships will be cherished forever.

Louis Yount
Hartsville, SC

DIJON SUPREME TURKEY BREASTS

1 (2-pound) boneless turkey breast, halved
Salt to taste
Pepper to taste
2 tablespoons butter
1 clove garlic, finely minced
1 tablespoon finely minced green onions
¼ pound mushrooms, sliced
¼ cup Dijon mustard
1 cup cream

Season turkey breast with salt and pepper. Heat butter in large skillet. Sauté turkey. When done, transfer to a warm platter. To pan drippings, add garlic, green onions, and mushrooms. Cook until onion is tender. Stir in mustard and cream. Simmer sauce until slightly thickened. Add turkey to sauce, turning to coat.
Serve over rice.
Yield: 4 servings

DRUM ROLL, PLEASE

PLEASE

Presenting the Whole Turkey:
Roasted, Fried, Smoked, Grilled

Peter Ring © 1995

I've got to hand it to the younger generation of Americans. They're healthier, smarter, better fed, better educated, and a whole lot better looking than the old turkey hunters I know. I like to hang out with young people because youth is where it's at. The future leaders of our country and the National Wild Turkey Federation—and, yes, the future stars of country music, too—are growing up around us every day, undetected. That's all the more reason to raise 'em right, to teach 'em right from wrong and, above all, to set a good example.

Porter Wagoner
Host of the Grand Ole Opry
Nashville, Tennessee

BAKED TURKEY

1 (12-pound) turkey
2 tablespoons salt
1½ teaspoons pepper
2 onions, chopped, divided
3 stalks celery, chopped, divided
3 cups water
¼ cup vegetable oil

Season turkey with salt and pepper. Place half the onion and celery into the cavity, and truss. Place remaining vegetables in bottom of roasting pan. Add water. Brush bird with oil; then set into pan atop vegetables. Bake at 300°, basting every 30 minutes, until joints move freely when twisted, about 4 hours. For a browner turkey, raise oven temperature to 400° 10 minutes before removing bird.
It may be necessary to add more water as turkey cooks.
Yield: 12 to 14 servings

BAKED WILD TURKEY

1 (15- to 20-pound) wild turkey
1 stick butter
Salt to taste
4 medium potatoes

Wash turkey with cold water. Dry. Sprinkle salt inside cavity. Rub entire turkey exterior with butter; sprinkle exterior with salt. Peel potatoes, place into cavity, and sew it closed. Place turkey inside large brown paper bag, and staple shut. Bake at 350° for 2 hours; then turn down oven to 250° and bake for 2 more hours.
Yield: 18 to 22 servings

Debbie LeCroy
Bradley, SC

WILEY D. TURKEY BAKED IN OVEN BAG

1 chicken bouillon cube
1 cup hot water
1 (12- to 16-pound) turkey
Prepared stuffing (optional)
Butter or margarine
Seasoned salt, as desired
1 tablespoon all-purpose flour
1 cup water or beer
1 apple, cored and sliced
1 orange, peeled and sectioned

Dissolve bouillon cube in water. Refrigerate bouillon until cold; then fill a syringe fitted with a large needle with bouillon. Inject bouillon into all meaty areas of turkey. Turkey may now be stuffed with your favorite stuffing, or left unstuffed. Rub turkey skin with butter or margarine; then sprinkle with seasoned salt. Shake flour inside oven bag. Place bag into a 13x9x2-inch baking pan; then place turkey in bag. Add water or beer; and apple and orange. Close turkey with nylon tie provided. Cut 6 half-inch slits in top of bag. Bake at 350° until thermometer inserted through slit in bag into the thickest part of the inner thigh, not touching bone, reads 180°.
Yield: 16 to 20 servings

Gary VanDyke
Vicksburg, MI

THANKSGIVING BAKED WILD TURKEY

1 (12-pound) wild turkey
Seasoned salt, as needed
Garlic salt, as needed
Salt, as needed
Pepper, as needed
4 stalks celery, cut into thirds
4 carrots, cut into thirds
3 medium onions, thickly sliced
4 bacon strips
Liquid margarine, as needed

Wash and clean turkey with cold water. Sprinkle turkey, inside and out, with seasoned salt and next 3 ingredients. Place turkey in cooking bag. Add celery, carrot, and onion to bag resting around turkey. Rest bacon across turkey. Squeeze margarine over entire turkey. Close bag and bake at 325° for 2 to 3 hours, or until meat thermometer inserted through a slit in bag into the thickest part of the inner thigh, not touching bone, reads 180°.
Yield: 12 to 14 servings

Sallie M. Phillips
Smith Mills, KY

SOUTHWESTERN-STYLE WILD TURKEY

1 (12- to 16-pound) wild turkey
2 cups Wild Turkey 101, divided
1 stick butter
1 medium onion, chopped
2 carrots, chopped
2 stalks celery, chopped
1 pound pecans, chopped
1 pound pitted prunes
4 apples, peeled and diced
2 stalks celery
2 cups water
1 cup honey

Wash turkey in cold water. Dry. Baste turkey with 1 cup Wild Turkey 101. Heat butter, and sauté chopped onion, carrot, and celery on low for 5 minutes. Add pecans, prunes, apples, and second cup of Wild Turkey 101. Mix thoroughly. Stuff turkey with this mixture. Lay 2 stalks celery on bottom of roasting pan, and add 2 cups water. Rest turkey on celery. Cover bird with foil, and bake at 350° for 3½ hours. Remove turkey, brush with honey, and bake 30 minutes longer.
Yield: 12 to 16 servings

Carlo Bruno
Palm Restaurant
Houston, TX

111

STUFFED MIDWESTERN WILD TURKEY

14 slices bacon, divided
1 cup chopped onion
¼ cup chopped celery
½ cup water
1 (8-ounce) package cornmeal stuffing mix
1 chicken bouillon cube
½ cup hot water
1 cup dry red wine, divided
1 (10- to 12-pound) wild turkey

Fry 8 slices bacon until crisp. Drain bacon, crumble, and set aside. Sauté onion and celery in bacon drippings. When vegetables are tender, add ½ cup water, and simmer for 5 minutes. Stir in stuffing mix and crumbled bacon. Dissolve bouillon cube in ½ cup hot water. Add ½ cup red wine to bouillon. Add bouillon-wine liquid to stuffing mixture, and stuff turkey. Transfer turkey to roasting pan. Lay 4 slices bacon across the breast, and wrap one slice bacon around each leg. Cover pan with foil; then place lid on pan. Bake in 300° oven for 4½ hours. Remove cover and foil. Pour remaining wine over turkey. Baste every 10 minutes while cooking an additional 40 minutes.
Yield: 12 to 15 servings

A. M. Glombowski
Lake Forest, IL

ROAST TURKEY

1 (10- to 12-pound) turkey
1 cup honey
1 cup apple cider syrup
3 large apples, cut into eighths

Wash turkey in cold water. Dry. Make several ½-inch slits into skin on thighs and breast. Loosen skin from meat. Mix honey with apple cider syrup. With a baster, insert honey-syrup mixture into the slits. Insert apples into the cavity. Place turkey on rack in covered roasting pan. Roast turkey, covered, at 350° for 15 minutes per pound, basting frequently. Uncover, and roast 20 minutes longer until browned.
Yield: 10 to 12 servings

Bill Devon
Weathersfield, VT

ROAST WILD TURKEY WITH ROSEMARY-GARLIC BUTTER

4 sticks unsalted butter
12 large garlic cloves, minced, divided
⅓ cup + ¼ cup rosemary or 4 tablespoons dried and crumbled
2 tablespoons coarse salt, divided
1 teaspoon freshly ground pepper, divided
3 tablespoons chopped sage or 1 tablespoon dried and crumbled
2 lemons, quartered
1 (12-pound) turkey
¾ cup peanut oil
2 cups chopped carrot
2 cups chopped onion
1 cup chopped celery
1 cup chicken or turkey stock
2 cups water
Salt to taste
Pepper to taste

In a medium saucepan, heat the butter, 8 minced garlic cloves, ⅓ cup rosemary (or 3 tablespoons dried), ½ teaspoon salt, and ½ teaspoon pepper until butter melts. Set aside. May be made up to 2 days in advance refrigerated; melt butter before using. Heat oven to 475°. Heat roasting pan in oven. Combine remaining garlic, rosemary, salt, and pepper with sage, and rub into cavity. Squeeze lemon juice into cavity; then place squeezed lemons into cavity. Truss turkey with string. Remove roasting pan from oven and brush with ¼ cup oil. Place turkey on side in roasting pan. Brush remaining oil on turkey. Roast 10 minutes, and remove from oven. Turn turkey onto other side, baste with some oil from pan, and place in oven for 10 minutes. Remove roasting pan from oven, and reduce heat to 250°. Turn turkey breast-side up. Return to oven, and roast, basting with butter mixture every 20 minutes. After 2½ hours, add carrot, onion, and celery to pan. Roast about 4 hours. Transfer turkey to platter. Add stock and 1 to 2 cups water to make gravy. Season to taste.
Yield: 12 to 14 servings

Jeffrey Johnson
Eugene, OR

One of the great things about The National Wild Turkey Federation's members is their spirit of intense, but friendly, competition to be the best and to do the most for the resource. Local volunteers are the heartbeat of the organization, and funding is its lifeblood. I have found through the years that the more we do, the more we get out of NWTF membership—and that holds true for a lot of good causes we Americans support.

Tom Muench
Tomah, WI

HONEY-BAKED
WILD TURKEY

1 (10-pound) wild turkey
6 tablespoons honey
1 teaspoon salt
1 teaspoon coarsely ground black pepper
¾ cup chopped onion
2 cups white wine
½ cup chicken broth
1 teaspoon parsley flakes
1 stick butter, melted
1 teaspoon Creole seasoning

Brush entire turkey with honey. (This works best if honey is warmed.) Salt and pepper turkey. Place on rack in large baking pan. Stuff turkey with your favorite stuffing. Mix onion, wine, broth, and parsley. Add butter and Creole seasoning. Baste bird with mixture. Place in oven and roast at 325° for 4 hours, occasionally basting with wine mixture.
Yield: 10 to 12 servings

TIPS FOR DEEP-FRYING A TURKEY

- Always make sure the turkey is thawed completely.
- Clean turkey in the same manner you would for roasting.
- Do not stuff the turkey when deep frying.
- Either inject turkey with liquid seasoning or rub dry seasonings inside and out. Some examples include:
  hot pepper sauce
  black pepper
  Italian dressing
  Cajun seasonings
  paprika
- To determine how much oil to use, first fill the pot with water and lower the turkey into it (water should cover turkey without spilling over; adjust water level accordingly. Remove the turkey and note how much water is in pot (or measure it). Discard water and fill pot with oil. Heat oil (to at least 310°) before adding turkey.
- A heavy wire coat hanger hooked to the band securing the drumsticks is a handy tool for lowering and raising the turkey.

Be careful during either procedure.

- Cooking time table:

  Skinless turkey—3 minutes per pound

  Turkey with skin—3½ minutes per pound
- Let turkey sit for 20 to 30 minutes before carving.
- Jamie offers his recipe for Cracker-Style Whole Fried Turkey on page 116.

Jamie Adams
Bushnell, FL

115

CRACKER-STYLE
WHOLE FRIED TURKEY

12 ounces Tabasco sauce
¼ cup cayenne pepper
¼ cup pepper
4 tablespoons paprika
Garlic salt, as needed
1 (12- to 14-pound) turkey
Peanut oil, as needed

Mix Tabasco sauce and next 4 ingredients. Rub inside and outside of turkey with Tabasco mixture. Fill cooker with oil (enough to completely immerse a 12- to 14-pound turkey), and heat to 310°. Carefully place bird in the cooker. Periodically check, using a candy thermometer, to ensure temperature remains constant. Cook turkey for 3½ minutes per pound or until it floats. Remove and drain on paper towels.
Can be wrapped in foil until served.
Yield: 14 to 18 servings

Jamie Adams
Bushnell, FL

WOODARDS' WILD TURKEY FRY

3 tablespoons liquid onion
¼ bottle liquid crab boil
¾ (16-ounce) bottle Italian dressing
2 tablespoons cayenne pepper
1 (12-pound) wild turkey
Salt to taste
Peanut oil
Crab boil packet

Mix first 4 ingredients. Store in refrigerator for up to 4 hours. The night before cooking the turkey, remove giblets, and coat with salt, if desired. Inject prepared mixture into thighs, drumsticks, wings, back, and breasts. Massage each injection point site in order to spread seasoning throughout body. Wire legs together. Wrap in plastic wrap and store in refrigerator overnight. Heat oil to 300°. Add crab boil packet to turkey cavity. Submerge turkey in oil. Cook 3½ to 4 minutes per pound. When turkey rises to the top of oil, remove from cooker and drain well.
Yield: 12 to 14 servings

James and Kathryn Woodard
Jacksonville, TX

EEJAY'S EASY DEEP-FRIED TURKEY

Salt, as desired
Pepper, as desired
Paprika, as desired
Garlic powder, as desired
Other seasonings, as desired
1 (12-pound) turkey
5 gallons peanut oil

Mix seasoning. Rub on outside and inside of turkey. Heat peanut oil to 310°, and deep fry, breast side down, 3 minutes per pound. Turn turkey over, and cook 1 minute longer or until thickest part of turkey registers 175° on meat thermometer. Remove, and cool.
Yield: 12 to 15 servings

Eejay Jones
Aiken, SC

MO'S DEEP-FRIED TURKEY

1 (6.4-ounce) jar Mo's Mix seasoned salt, divided
4 sticks butter, melted
5 to 10 gallons peanut oil
1 (9-pound) turkey

Combine ¼ cup seasoned salt with butter. Rub outside of turkey with the salt-butter mixture. Sprinkle turkey cavity with remaining seasoned salt, imbedding it into meat. Heat oil in a very large (10- to 15-gallon) cast iron cooking pot until it is nearly smoking. Very carefully submerge turkey into oil. Cook for approximately 3½ to 4 minutes per pound, or until meat thermometer inserted between 4 to 6 inches into breast reads 185°.
Yield: 10 to 12 servings

Mo Skaggs
Rolla, MO

MO'S DEEP-FRIED TURKEY II

16 cups water
2 cups Mo's Mix seasoned salt
8 tablespoons soy sauce
4 tablespoons Worcestershire sauce
1 (15-pound) turkey
5 to 10 gallons peanut oil

Mix water with next 3 ingredients. Place turkey into a very large container with an airtight lid. Pour marinade over turkey. Cover tightly, and marinate at least 12 hours, or overnight, turning frequently. Heat oil in a very large (10- to 15-gallon) cast iron cooking pot until nearly smoking. Very carefully submerge turkey into oil. Cook for approximately 3½ to 4 minutes per pound, or until meat thermometer inserted between 4 to 6 inches into breast reads 185°.
Yield: 15 to 20 servings

Mo Skaggs
Rolla, MO

FRIED WHOLE TURKEY

Salt, as needed
Pepper, as needed
Paprika, as needed
1 (12-pound) whole turkey
5 gallons peanut oil

Thaw turkey and remove giblets. Sprinkle bird generously with salt, pepper, and paprika. Remove excess skin. In a pot large enough to submerge turkey, heat peanut oil to 375°. Tie legs together, and tie wings to body with heavy-duty string. Cook turkey 3½ to 4 minutes per pound, or until it floats, shifting it frequently to prevent burning.
Yield: 12 to 14 servings

Sessions Company
Enterprise, AL

CAJUN DEEP-FRIED WILD TURKEY

1 (10- to 15-pound) wild turkey
5 gallons peanut oil
2 tablespoons Cajun seasoning
1 stick butter or margarine
½ teaspoon garlic powder
½ teaspoon cayenne pepper (optional)

Pour peanut oil into a 10-gallon pot. Place pot on propane fish cooker burner and heat oil to 375°. Dry turkey thoroughly. Tie two cotton strings around the carcass so bird can easily be lifted out of oil. Carefully submerge turkey in oil. Deep fry for 3½ to 4½ minutes per pound and cook until turkey floats to the top. Remove bird from oil, and immediately dust heavily with Cajun seasoning. Melt butter or margarine, and add garlic powder and cayenne, if desired. Allow turkey to cool slightly before carving. Brush with seasoned butter, if desired.
Yield: 12 to 16 servings

Steve Cole
Perryville, AR

FRIED WILD TURKEY

1 (24-ounce) bottle Italian salad dressing
1 (10- to 15-pound) wild turkey
5 gallons peanut oil

Strain salad dressing to remove solids. With a large syringe, inject salad dressing into turkey. Refrigerate turkey 24 hours. Heat oil to 300° on the outdoor frier. Insert a coat hanger inside the carcass, and hang it over a metal rod to suspend it in the hot oil. Cook 3½ minutes per pound.
Slice turkey very thin and serve with wild rice and your choice of vegetables.

Dale Bounds
Lufkin, TX

WHOLE DEEP-FRIED TURKEY

1 (8-ounce) bottle Italian dressing, strained
2 tablespoons garlic juice
1 teaspoon salt
1 teaspoon cayenne pepper
1 teaspoon pepper
1 (12- to 16-pound) turkey
5 gallons peanut oil

Mix the dressing and next 4 ingredients. Pour into an 8-ounce jar, discarding excess. Use a baster with needle attachment to inject marinade into the turkey, with the majority going into the breast. Heat oil in large, 18- to 20-quart pot to 350°. Immerse turkey very carefully, ensuring oil doesn't spill over sides, and fry about 50 minutes, or until tender. Carefully lift turkey from pot, and drain on newspaper or paper towels.
Yield: 14 to 20 servings

Tom Huhmann
Tipton, MO

BASIC CREOLE FRIED TURKEY

1 (12- to 14-pound) turkey
2 teaspoons seasoned salt
1 teaspoon pepper
1 teaspoon cayenne pepper
2 large onions
1 stalk celery
1 small bell pepper
2 cloves garlic
3 jalapeño peppers, or other hot peppers
5 gallons oil

Rinse turkey in cold water, and pat dry. Mix together seasoned salt
and next two ingredients. Rub turkey inside and out with seasoning
mixture. Grind onion and next 4 ingredients in food processor, and
stuff into cavity. Wrap turkey in foil, and refrigerate at least 12 hours,
or overnight. Heat oil until nearly smoking. Fry turkey for 1 hour, or
until tender. Drain.
Yield: 14 to 18 servings

Jim Cupit
Hermitage, TN

HICKORY-SMOKED TURKEY

2 cups hickory or apple chips
1 (6- to 8-pound turkey)

Soak chips in water for at least 1 hour. Rinse turkey in cold water, and
dry thoroughly. Fold wings close to the body, and tie or skewer. Close
both openings with skewers, and tie legs together tightly, Insert spit
rod through the center of the cavity, balancing carefully. Secure with
holding forks. Smoke over low, indirect heat with a water pan
underneath. Throw half of the drained wood chips on the hot coals.
Keep the lid down, and cook for approximately 5 to 6 hours. Add
remaining chips as needed. Let turkey rest 10 minutes before carving.
Yield: 8 to 10 servings

Masterbuilt Manufacturing, Inc.
Columbus, GA

SMOKED TURKEY

1 (12-pound) turkey
¼ cup vegetable oil
¼ cup dry red wine
⅓ cup fresh lemon juice
2 tablespoons butter
1 tablespoon Worcestershire sauce
1 teaspoon marjoram
1 clove garlic, minced
Salt to taste
Pepper to taste

Rinse turkey in cold water. Mix oil and next 8 ingredients. Rub turkey inside and out with oil-wine mixture. Pour remaining mixture into a water pan, and fill with water. Smoke turkey for 8 to 12 hours, keeping pan filled with water.
Yield: 12 to 14 servings

Mrs. James C. Garland, III
Sapulpa, OK

SMOKED DRAMBUIE TURKEY

1 (12-pound) turkey
½ cup melted butter
½ cup maple syrup
⅓ cup Drambuie (liqueur)

Rinse turkey and pat dry. Heat butter, maple syrup, and Drambuie in a small saucepan. With a large syringe, inject half the butter mixture into the turkey. Brush the remaining mixture over the turkey. Insert a meat thermometer into the thickest part of the inner thigh, and place on smoker filled with 12 pounds charcoal; 3 to 4 sticks of wood from a fruit, mesquite, or hickory tree; and a pan with 8 quarts hot water. Replenish water as needed. Smoke for 6 to 8 hours, or until thermometer reads 180°.
Yield: 12 to 15 servings

Sean Burke
Augusta, GA

SMOKED ROSEMARY-BRANDY TURKEY

1 lemon, halved
2 tablespoons brandy
1 teaspoon Dijon mustard
1 teaspoon dried rosemary
2 tablespoons honey
Salt to taste
Pepper to taste
1 onion, studded with whole cloves
1 (9-pound) turkey

Squeeze juice of lemon half into a shallow dish, and mix in next 6 ingredients for marinade. Add other lemon half and onion into cavity. Refrigerate turkey 2 hours in marinade. Place turkey on top rack of smoker, and cover. After 15 minutes, baste with remaining marinade. Smoke 5 to 6 hours, or until meat thermometer reads 185°.
Yield: 10 to 12 servings

Masterbuilt Manufacturing Inc.
Columbus, GA

CHARCOAL-GRILLED WILD TURKEY

1 (12-pound) wild turkey

On a covered grill, place 15 charcoal briquets on each side of the pan. Ignite, and burn until coals are completely gray. Place a drip pan above charcoal with a grill above it. Place turkey in center of grill. Cover grill. Cook for approximately 3 hours, adding charcoal as necessary, basting frequently with drippings.
Yield: 12 to 14 servings

Jennifer Nannery
Sebago Lake, ME

GRILLED TURKEY BREAST MARINADE

1 cup soy sauce
1 cup teriyaki sauce
1 teaspoon Tabasco sauce
1 cup white wine
3 bay leaves
½ cup freshly grated ginger
6 garlic cloves, crushed
I lemon, juiced

Combine all ingredients. Marinate turkey breast 24 hours before grilling.
Yield: about 4 cups

Michael M. Tull
Roswell, GA

MARINADE FOR WILD TURKEY

1 cup peanut oil
¼ cup lemon juice
1 cup orange juice
½ cup white wine vinegar
1 small onion, chopped
1 teaspoon lemon pepper
1 teaspoon dried parsley
1 teaspoon Italian seasoning

Mix all ingredients.
Cut ½-inch turkey breast slices and place in bowl or in 2-gallon zip-top plastic bag. Pour entire mixture over turkey. Marinate at least 3 hours or overnight.
Yield: about 3 cups

Nancy Barber
Pompano Beach, FL

LEMON BARBECUE SAUCE

1 stick margarine
1 garlic clove, minced
4 teaspoons cornstarch
⅔ cup water
1 tablespoon sugar
½ teaspoon pepper
⅔ cup lemon juice
¼ teaspoon Tabasco sauce
½ teaspoon dried thyme
¼ cup vinegar

Melt margarine in saucepan; then sauté garlic until fragrant, about 1 to
2 minutes. Stir in cornstarch, then water. When thoroughly
combined, add remaining ingredients. Stir until slightly thickened.
Great poured over yellow rice and topped with Parmesan cheese.
Yield: 2 cups

Rosalie Kennamer
Auburn, AL

NO HUHU, ALL-KINE
HAWAIIAN MARINADE

1 cup macadamia nut oil, or olive oil
2 cups pineapple wine, or red wine
1 cup chopped onion
1 cup chopped carrot
1 cup chopped celery
4 cloves garlic, crushed
1 tablespoon peppercorns
6 bay leaves
8 cloves
½ teaspoon dried rosemary
¼ teaspoon whole thyme
¼ teaspoon oregano

Combine all ingredients. Marinate turkey, refrigerated, for 48 to 72
hours.
Yield: about 4 cups

Deane Gonzalez
Honolulu, HI

BENTON
MARINADE AND SAUCE

1 teaspoon garlic salt
1½ teaspoons dry mustard
¼ teaspoon pepper
2 tablespoons vegetable oil
¾ cup water
2 tablespoons soy sauce
3 tablespoons honey
1 tablespoon vinegar
1½ teaspoons celery seed
½ teaspoon ginger

Combine all ingredients in a saucepan, and simmer for 30 minutes.
Use as a turkey marinade, or serve as a sauce to accompany turkey.
Yield: about 2 cups

Mike Spence
Benton, IL

BASTING SAUCE FOR
GRILLED TURKEY

1 cup teriyaki sauce
1 cup soy sauce
1 stick butter

Heat teriyaki sauce, soy sauce, and butter, until butter melts. Use to
baste turkey while grilling.
Yield: 2½ cups

Rich and Judy Krona
Santa Rosa, CA

BARBECUE SAUCE

1 (32-ounce) bottle steak sauce
1½ cups tomato sauce
½ cup cider vinegar
½ cup Worcestershire sauce
½ cup pure maple syrup or honey
2 tablespoons brown mustard
2 tablespoons fresh horseradish, grated, or prepared
1 teaspoon Tabasco sauce

Combine all ingredients. Refrigerate until needed. Keeps 2 to 3 months.
Yield: 3½ pints

Mary Harris
Makanda, IL

TURKEY BARBECUE SAUCE

1 clove garlic, crushed
½ cup dried onion
1 teaspoon prepared mustard
2 tablespoons lemon juice
2 tablespoons brown sugar
½ cup crushed pineapple
1 cup ketchup or tomato sauce
½ teaspoon Worcestershire sauce
Salt, as needed
Pepper, as needed

Combine all ingredients thoroughly. Brush on turkey while cooking or serve with turkey for dipping.
Yield: about 2 cups

Neil Cost
Greenwood, SC

WILD TURKEY BOURBON SAUCE
(FOR BONELESS GAME)

1 large onion, sliced
1 stick butter
2 slices bacon, cut into 1-inch pieces
2 tablespoons garlic
2 cups sliced mushrooms
2 cans cream of mushroom soup
½ soup can Wild Turkey Bourbon
½ soup can red wine (any variety)

Sauté onion, butter, bacon, garlic and mushrooms in a large sauce pan. Cook only until bacon starts to brown on edges. Salt and pepper to taste, but take it very easy on the salt. Add remaining ingredients, reduce heat, and simmer 10 minutes. Adjust seasonings.

Baste meat with sauce, adding water if sauce becomes too thick.

John L. Morris
Bass Pro Shops
Springfield, MO

COALFIELD BARBECUE SAUCE

1¼ cups ketchup
1 cup brown sugar
1 tablespoon Worcestershire sauce
1 tablespoon mustard
1 tablespoon vinegar
1 tablespoon dried onion
2 teaspoon barbecue seasoning
1 teaspoon garlic powder
½ teaspoon hot sauce

Heat all ingredients in a saucepan, and simmer for 30 minutes or until sauce thickens.
Serve with grilled turkey.
Yield: about 3 cups

Mike Spence
Benton, IL

HOMEMADE
BARBECUE SAUCE

1 (32-ounce) bottle barbecue sauce
2 lemons, juiced
2 cups ketchup
1 tablespoon soy sauce
1 cup hickory-flavor barbecue sauce
2 cups brown sugar
1 cup sugar
½ cup vinegar
4 cups water
½ teaspoon onion juice
½ teaspoon garlic powder
1 stick butter

Combine all ingredients and simmer for 1 hour, or until sauce thickens. Serve with grilled turkey.
Yield: 2½ quarts

Richard Barkoskie
Jacksonville, FL

I n the twilight of my life, and always through my life, I've associated with kids. Right now I'm to the point where I try to help kids more than I do anything—photograph turkeys and help kids. I do think that the National Wild Turkey Federation's JAKES program is an excellent program for teaching.

Glenn C. "Tink" Smith
Piedmont, WV

TURKEY MARINADE

⅓ cup Worcestershire sauce
⅓ cup soy sauce
⅓ cup teriyaki sauce
Dash of red wine
5 tablespoons oil
½ teaspoon onion juice
½ teaspoon garlic juice
1 tablespoon minced garlic

Thoroughly mix all ingredients.
Pour over turkey breasts and let soak at least 6 hours, or overnight, turning frequently.
Yield: about 1½ cups

GOBBLE UP THE LEFTOVERS

From Casseroles and Chilis to Meatballs and Croquettes

Until there's a war or some other national emergency, most people tend to take their country and their freedoms for granted. I can tell you this: Every soldier, sailor, marine, and airman who has served in combat knows the terrible cost of freedom.

America is still a relatively young nation—an experiment, more or less. I hope the spirit of independence will inspire us to preserve what we have bought and paid for in blood since we declared ourselves a nation in 1776. The National Wild Turkey Federation's regard for God and country keeps its mission focused on the real values that have made America great.

William G. Smith
WWII Veteran
Edgefield, SC

TURKEY POCKETS

1 (3-ounce) package cream cheese, softened
2 tablespoons margarine
2 cups cooked, cubed turkey
¼ teaspoon salt
⅛ teaspoon pepper
2 tablespoons milk
1 tablespoon chopped onion
1 tablespoon chopped pimento, optional
1 (8-ounce) can crescent rolls
1 tablespoon melted butter

Blend cream cheese and margarine until smooth. Add turkey and next 4 ingredients, and pimento, if desired. Separate dough into 4 rectangles. Sealing perforations. Spoon ½ cup turkey mixture into center of each rectangle. Pull the 4 corners of each piece to center, and seal. Brush each piece with butter. Place on ungreased cookie sheet. Bake at 400° for 15 minutes.
Yield: 4 servings

132

TURKEY DIVINE

1 bunch broccoli
Salt to taste
Nonstick cooking spray
4 cups cooked turkey pieces
1 cup mayonnaise
2 (10¾-ounce) cans cream of chicken soup
1 teaspoon lemon juice
½ teaspoon curry powder
½ cup grated sharp Cheddar cheese
½ cup breadcrumbs
1 tablespoon margarine, melted

Steam broccoli in salted water until crisp-tender. Drain. Coat a 2-quart baking dish with nonstick cooking spray. Arrange broccoli in casserole. Place turkey over broccoli. Combine mayonnaise and next 4 ingredients; pour over turkey. Mix breadcrumbs and margarine; sprinkle on top. Bake at 350° for 30 to 40 minutes, or until bubbly. *Serve with cornbread or over biscuits or rice.*
Yield: 6 to 8 servings

John Webb
Jackson, TN

MISS HELEN'S GOULASH

1 pound ground turkey
1 medium onion, chopped
1 (10¾-ounce) can tomato soup
1 (soup) can water
About 6 ounces medium egg noodles
1 (14¾-ounce) can cream-style corn
1 (2¼-ounce) can sliced black olives, optional
Nonstick cooking spray
4 slices American cheese

Brown the turkey and onion. Add soup and water. Bring to a boil; add noodles. Simmer until noodles are tender, about 20 minutes. Add corn, and olives, if desired. Coat a 2-quart casserole with nonstick cooking spray. Pour turkey mixture into casserole. Top with cheese. Bake at 325° for 30 minutes, or when cheese melts.
Yield: 4 servings

Helen "Mom" Rosenlieb
Clay City, IL

PRIZE TURKEY

½ stick butter
1 pound mushrooms, stemmed and sliced
½ cup diced celery
1 small onion, diced
4 tablespoons flour
1½ cups half-and-half
2 cups cooked, cubed turkey
½ teaspoon salt
Large pinch of freshly ground pepper
1 (16-ounce) package spaghetti, broken into small pieces
2 cups grated Cheddar cheese

In large skillet, melt the butter and sauté mushroom, celery, and onion. In a cup, combine the flour with a little water to form a paste. Pour half-and-half into a bowl and incorporate flour mixture into it. Add flour mixture to vegetables, and heat, stirring constantly, until thickened. Add the turkey, salt, and pepper. Cook spaghetti until tender. Drain. Add spaghetti to turkey mixture. Transfer to a 2-quart baking dish and top with cheese. Bake at 350° until cheese melts.
Yield: 8 servings

Sam Mars
Harrogate, TN

OVEN-BAKED TURKEY

1 (12-pound) turkey, cut into serving pieces
Salt to taste
Cayenne pepper to taste
2½ sticks butter, melted, divided
½ teaspoon angostura bitters
2 cups seasoned breadcrumbs

Season turkey with salt and cayenne pepper. Pour two-thirds of butter into a bowl. Add bitters, and mix well. Dip turkey pieces in butter-bitters mixture; then roll in breadcrumbs. Grease a baking pan. Place turkey in pan, and drizzle with half the remaining butter; sprinkle with remaining crumbs. Cover pan with foil. Bake at 350° for 1 hour. Uncover and pour remaining butter over turkey. Bake, uncovered, for 30 to 45 minutes, or until tender and brown.
Yield: 10 to 12 servings

Sean Burke
Augusta, GA

BROWNED AND STEAMED TURKEY

1 (8-pound) turkey, cut into bite-size pieces
½ cup flour
Salt and pepper to taste
4 tablespoons oil
8 to 12 mushrooms, sliced
¼ cup water

MILK GRAVY

2 cups milk, divided
¼ cup flour

Preheat oven to 350°. Dip turkey pieces in mixture of flour, salt, and pepper. Brown in hot oil. Remove from pan. Drain on paper towels. Place in greased baking dish; add mushrooms and ¼ cup water. Cover and bake for 1 hour. Remove turkey and mushrooms from baking dish. Pour in 1½ cups milk and scrape bottom and sides of skillet. Mix ½ cup milk and ¼ cup flour together; stir well. Bring milk in baking dish to a boil; slowly add flour mixture. (Add extra flour or milk as needed to get the right thickness desired.)
Serve over wild rice or potatoes.
Yield: 6 to 8 servings

Bill Stevens
Federal Cartridge Co.
Anoka, MN

TURKEY AND VEGETABLE STIR-FRY

7 teaspoons vegetable oil, divided
2 medium carrots, julienned
5 large mushrooms, stemmed, thinly sliced
½ pound snow peas
1 tablespoon grated fresh ginger
2 teaspoons minced garlic
3 cups cooked shredded dark turkey meat
⅓ cup turkey or chicken broth
2 tablespoons soy sauce
¾ cup thinly sliced green onions, divided
2 teaspoons sesame oil
1 tablespoon chopped cilantro or parsley

Heat 1 tablespoon oil over medium heat in large nonstick skillet. Add carrot; sauté for 1 minute. Add mushroom; cook, shaking skillet and stirring, for 2 minutes. Empty vegetables into a large bowl. Heat 1 tablespoon oil into skillet; add snow peas and cook for 1 minute longer. Transfer to cooked vegetables. Heat remaining oil; add ginger and garlic, and cook 15 seconds. Add turkey, broth, and soy sauce. Stir-fry 1½ minutes. Return vegetables to skillet Add ½ cup green onions, and sesame oil. Toss well; cook 1 minute. Remove to platter, garnish with remaining green onions; top with cilantro or parsley.
Yield: 4 to 6 servings

Missouri Poultry Federation
Columbia, MO

136

WILD TURKEY À LA KING

¼ cup sliced mushrooms
2 tablespoons butter
4½ teaspoons all-purpose flour
¼ teaspoon salt
1 teaspoon Worcestershire sauce
1 cup milk
¼ cup chopped bell pepper
¼ cup chopped pimento-stuffed olives
1 cup cooked diced wild turkey
2 slices hot toast

Sauté mushrooms in butter for 5 minutes. Add flour, salt, and Worcestershire. Blend in milk, and cook until thickened, stirring constantly. Add bell pepper, olives, and turkey. Heat thoroughly. Serve on toast.
Yield: 2 servings

Liz Szefcyk
Amherst, OH

CREAMED WILD TURKEY

2 cups turkey broth
1 cup water
4 tablespoons flour
4 tablespoons butter
2 cups cooked cubed wild turkey
Salt and pepper to taste
4 hot biscuits, halved

Boil broth and water; set aside. In a large skillet heat flour and butter; slowly add 2 cups broth mixture till creamy. Then add turkey and stir well. Slowly add rest of broth mixture and cook on low for 10 minutes. Season with salt and pepper. Split biscuits and pour creamed turkey over biscuits.
To serve, mound mashed potatoes on a large platter; surround with biscuits and top with creamed turkey.
Yield: 4 servings

Juanita Colvin
Craigsville, VA

BAKED TURKEY AND RICE CASSEROLE

1 (10¾-ounce) can cream of celery soup
1 (10¾-ounce) can cream of mushroom soup
2 soup cans milk
2 cups rice
4 cups chopped uncooked turkey
1 (1.15-ounce) envelope onion soup mix

Into a 3-quart baking dish, combine both soups, milk, and rice. Top with turkey. Sprinkle with onion soup mix. Cover with foil. Bake at 325° for 2 to 2½ hours, or until turkey is tender.
Yield: 4 to 6 servings

Sean Burke
Augusta, GA

TURKEY FRIED RICE

6 teaspoons vegetable oil, divided
1 small bell pepper, chopped
1 small onion, chopped
2 carrots, sliced
1 cup broccoli florets
2 eggs
1 cup diced turkey
Soy sauce, as needed
2 cups cooked rice

Heat wok. Add 2 teaspoons oil. Add pepper, and next 3 ingredients. Cook until crisp-tender. Remove, and set aside. Add 2 teaspoons oil to wok. Add eggs, scramble, remove; set aside. Add remaining oil. Add turkey, and stir-fry until cooked, about 10 minutes. Add soy sauce to taste. Return vegetables and eggs to wok. Add rice and additional soy sauce, as desired. Mix thoroughly.
Yield: 6 servings

Jacqueline Langston
Edgefield, SC

138

TURKEY HASH

½ cup all-purpose flour
1½ tablespoons bacon drippings
6 tablespoons butter
3 cups chopped onion
2 cups chopped celery
1 cup chopped bell pepper
1 cup chopped parsley
2 cups chopped green onions
1 tablespoon chopped garlic
½ large lemon, chopped
½ teaspoon dried mint
¼ teaspoon angostura bitters
3 tablespoons Worcestershire sauce
2 teaspoons Tabasco sauce
1 cup chopped cooked carrots
3 cups chopped cooked potatoes
Water, as needed
6 cups cooked turkey
1 cup white wine
Salt to taste

Make a brown roux with the flour, bacon drippings, and butter. Add onion, celery, and bell pepper. Simmer until tender. Stir in parsley, and next 2 ingredients. Simmer until tender. Add lemon, next 6 ingredients, and a little water. Simmer 15 minutes. Pour mixture into a 3-quart baking dish. Add turkey, wine, salt to taste, and enough water to almost cover. Bake at 350° for 35 minutes or until brown and not too dry.
Serve over biscuits or toast.
Yield: 6 to 8 servings

Sean Burke
Augusta, GA

TEXAS TURKEY BARBECUE

¾ cup tomato juice
¼ cup ketchup
8 teaspoons vinegar
2 tablespoons molasses
4½ teaspoons Worcestershire sauce
1 tablespoon dried onion flakes
1 tablespoon sugar
2 teaspoons paprika
¾ teaspoon salt
¾ teaspoon dry mustard
½ teaspoon chili powder
½ teaspoon dried garlic flakes
½ teaspoon cayenne pepper
Dash of Tabasco sauce
2 cups grilled minced turkey
4 hamburger buns, split and toasted

In 3-quart saucepan over high heat, combine tomato juice and next 13 ingredients, and bring to a boil. Reduce heat, and simmer 10 minutes. Add turkey, and simmer 10 to 15 minutes, or until hot. Serve on buns.
Yield: 4 servings

Terry Steele
Homosassa, FL

HOT TAMALE TURKEY LOAF

2 pounds ground turkey breast
2 cups soft breadcrumbs
2 eggs, lightly beaten
½ cup milk
1 medium onion, chopped
1 teaspoon cumin
1 teaspoon salt
¼ teaspoon freshly ground black pepper
2 cups medium-hot chunky salsa, drained
2 cups shredded Monterey Jack cheese, divided

In large bowl, combine turkey and next 7 ingredients. On (12x15-inch) sheet of plastic wrap, form turkey mixture into (9x12-inch) rectangle. Spoon salsa over meat to within ½ inch of edges. Top with 1½ cups cheese. Starting at narrow side, roll jelly-roll style. Using plastic wrap as carrier, place loaf in ungreased 13x9x2-inch roasting pan, seam side down; remove plastic wrap. Bake at 350° for 60 to 90 minutes, or until thermometer, inserted into center, registers 160° to 165°, and juices run clear when knife is inserted near the center. Top with remaining cheese, and bake 1 to 2 minutes until cheese melts.
Yield: 8 servings

National Turkey Federation
Reston, VA

ROLAND'S WILD TURKEY ENCHILADAS

1 medium onion, chopped
½ cup chopped celery
2 cups wild turkey, cooked and chopped
Dash of cumin
1 (10¾-ounce) can cream of chicken soup
1 (10¾-ounce) can cream of mushroom soup
1 (4-ounce) can chopped green chiles
1 (16-ounce) carton sour cream
2 cups Monterey Jack cheese
2 cups Cheddar cheese
1 package 12 corn tortillas
1 (4-ounce) can sliced black olives, drained
1 bunch chopped green onions, optional

Sauté onion and celery in a skillet until clear. Add chopped turkey and cumin to taste; set aside. Combine soups, chiles, and sour cream; set aside. Grate cheeses. Steam tortillas or wrap several at a time in a damp paper towel and microwave for 30 seconds. Assemble tortillas using about ¼ cup turkey, 2 tablespoons soup mix, and 2 tablespoons mixed cheeses. Roll tightly and place in a 3-quart baking dish, placing seam side down. Mix black olives with remaining soup; then pour over enchiladas. Top with green onions, if desired. Cover with remaining cheese. Bake at 350° until bubbly.
Yield: 6 servings

Roland J. Castanic II
Texas City, TX

TURKEY ENCHILADAS

2 (10¾-ounce) cans cream of mushroom soup
½ cup sour cream
½ cup diced green chiles
12 tortillas, flour or corn
1 cup grated Monterey Jack cheese
1 cup Cheddar cheese
½ cup chopped onion
2 cups cooked cubed wild turkey
Nonstick cooking spray

Combine soup, sour cream, and chiles. Heat thoroughly. Warm tortillas in damp towel in microwave. Coat a 13x9x2-inch baking pan with nonstick cooking spray. Mix cheeses, onion, turkey, and 1 cup soup mixture. Put 2 tablespoons of cheese-turkey mixture in center of each tortilla. Roll tortillas and place in baking dish. Pour remaining soup mixture over top. Cover, and bake at 350° for 30 minutes. *Uncover, and top with sliced ripe olives and additional cheese, if desired.*
Yield: 4 to 5 servings

Diana Showalter
Roann, IN

TURKEY ENCHILADA CASSEROLE

Nonstick cooking spray, as needed
2 (10¾-ounce) cans cream of chicken soup
1 (10¾-ounce) can cream of mushroom soup
1 (4-ounce) can whole green chilies
1 large onion, chopped
12 corn tortillas
2 cups shredded cooked turkey
1 pound Monterey Jack cheese
½ cup slightly crushed tortilla chips, optional

Coat casserole dish lightly with nonstick cooking spray. In medium bowl, mix soups, chilies, and onion. Into the casserole, layer tortillas, turkey, soup mixture, and cheese. Top with tortilla chips if desired. Bake at 350° for 50 to 60 minutes.
Yield: 4 to 6 servings

Jeffrey Johnson
Eugene, OR

WILD RICE AND TURKEY CASSEROLE

1 cup wild rice
4 cups boiling water
1 pound mushrooms, sliced
1 medium onion, chopped
6 tablespoons butter, divided
2 teaspoons salt
¼ teaspoon freshly ground pepper
3 cups diced wild turkey
½ cup sliced blanched almonds
3 cups turkey or chicken broth
1½ cups heavy cream
3 tablespoons Parmesan cheese

Soak rice in water for 1 hour. Drain. Sauté mushroom and onion in 1 tablespoon butter until tender, about 8 to 10 minutes. Grease a 3-quart casserole with 1 tablespoon butter, and add rice, mushroom-onion mixture, salt and next 3 ingredients. Lightly fold in broth and cream. Cover, and bake at 350° for 1½ hours. Remove cover, sprinkle with Parmesan, and dot with remaining butter. Raise oven temperature to 450° and bake for an additional 5 minutes.
Yield: 6 to 8 servings

Timothy D. Skidmore
Bellefontaine, OH

TURKEY BROCCOLI CASSEROLE

1½ cups prepared stuffing
Nonstick cooking spray
2½ cups cooked cubed turkey
2 chicken bouillon cubes
1¼ cups hot water
2 tablespoons all-purpose flour
¼ cup water
1 (10-ounce) package frozen chopped broccoli, cooked and drained
¼ cup sour cream
4 slices American cheese, halved diagonally

Spoon stuffing into a casserole coated with nonstick cooking spray. Top with turkey. Dissolve bouillon cubes in water. Shake flour and water; mix into hot bouillon. Heat liquid on low, stirring constantly, until thickened. Combine broccoli with sour cream. Incorporate with hot liquid; pour over turkey. Bake at 350° for 15 minutes. Top with cheese triangles, and bake another 5½ minutes, or until cheese melts.
Yield: 4 servings

Col. Jim Newbill
Atlanta, GA

TURKEY-TOMATO BAKE

½ cup chopped onion
½ cup chopped celery
1 tablespoon butter
1 (15.25-ounce) can whole kernel corn, drained
1½ cups cooked cubed turkey
1 (10¾-ounce) can tomato soup
⅓ cup ketchup
6 ounces shredded American cheese
2 cups frozen crinkle-cut potatoes

In a skillet, sauté onion and celery in butter until tender. Stir in corn and next 4 ingredients. Transfer to an 8x8x2-inch square baking pan. Arrange potatoes over top. Bake, uncovered, at 425° for 25 minutes.
Yield: 4 servings

VerDonna Otey
Makanda, IL

TURKETTI

1½ cups spaghetti, broken into 2-inch pieces
2 cups diced cooked turkey
¼ cup diced pimento
½ cup chopped onion
¼ cup chopped bell pepper
1 (10¾-ounce) can cream of celery soup
½ cup turkey broth
½ teaspoon salt
½ teaspoon pepper
1½ cups Parmesan cheese, divided

Cook spaghetti. Drain. Mix turkey and next 8 ingredients in a large bowl. Stir in 1 cup cheese and the spaghetti. Pour into casserole. Top with remaining cheese. Bake at 325° for 45 minutes.
Yield: 4 to 6 servings

Rose Dameron
Lexington, NC

TURKETTY

1½ cups macaroni
2 cups cooked diced turkey
1 onion, diced
½ cup diced bell pepper
½ cup diced pimento
½ teaspoon pepper
1 (10¾-ounce) can cream of mushroom soup
1 cup turkey or chicken stock
1½ cups Cheddar cheese

Cook macaroni. Drain. Mix macaroni and next 7 ingredients. Place in a 3-quart baking dish; cover with foil. Bake at 300° for 40 minutes. Remove foil. Top with cheese. Continue baking until cheese melts.
Yield: 4 servings

Mike Halter
East Ridge, TN

EASY MICROWAVE TURKEY LASAGNA

1 pound ground turkey breast
1 clove garlic, chopped
1 cup chopped onion
1 (16-ounce) can tomatoes, chopped, liquid reserved
1 (6-ounce) can tomato paste
2½ teaspoons Italian seasoning or oregano
Nonstick cooking spray
8 lasagna noodles, uncooked
1 (12-ounce) carton reduced-fat cottage cheese
2 cups shredded mozzarella cheese

In 2-quart casserole, combine turkey, garlic, and onion. Cover.
Microwave on High for 2½ minutes. Stir. Cook on High an additional
2½ minutes. Stir in tomatoes and liquid, tomato paste, and seasoning.
Microwave, uncovered, on High for 5 minutes. Lightly coat a 2-quart
rectangular casserole with nonstick cooking spray. Spoon one-third of
sauce (about 1⅓ cups) into casserole. Top with 4 lasagna noodles.
Spoon cottage cheese over noodles. Sprinkle mozzarella cheese on top;
then one-third more sauce. Top with remaining noodles. Spoon
remaining sauce over noodles, and cover with vented plastic wrap.
Microwave on High for 5 minutes. Reduce to Medium power, and
cook 20 to 25 minutes, or until noodles are tender.
*Place several layers of paper towels in bottom of microwave to absorb
spillovers.*
Yield: 8 servings

Missouri Poultry Federation
Columbia, MO

TURKEY POTATO LASAGNA

1 pound ground turkey breast
1 (10- ounce) can diced tomatoes and green chiles
½ cup chopped onion
1 (10-ounce) package chopped broccoli, thawed
1 (15-ounce) carton nonfat ricotta cheese
1 teaspoon basil
1 teaspoon salt
1 teaspoon pepper
Nonstick cooking spray
3 medium baking potatoes, sliced lengthwise, divided
1½ cups shredded low-fat mozzarella cheese
½ cup Parmesan cheese

In a large skillet over medium-high heat, sauté turkey 5 to 6 minutes, or until no longer pink. Drain. Stir in tomatoes and onion. Simmer 5 to 7 minutes, or until heated throughout. In medium bowl, combine broccoli and next 4 ingredients. Coat a 13x9x2-inch rectangular pan with nonstick cooking spray. Add one-third of the potatoes. Top with half the turkey mixture and half the broccoli mixture; sprinkle with half the mozzarella cheese, and repeat layers. Top with remaining potato slices. Sprinkle with Parmesan cheese. Cover with foil, and bake at 350° for 30 minutes. Uncover, and bake an additional 55 to 60 minutes, or until potatoes are tender and top is brown.
Cool 10 minutes before serving.
Yield: 8 servings

National Turkey Federation
Reston, VA

TURKEY SWISS PIE

1 (9-inch) pie shell
1½ cups diced cooked wild turkey
½ cup sliced onion
1 cup shredded Swiss cheese
3 eggs, lightly beaten
1 cup mayonnaise
½ cup milk

In pie shell, layer turkey, onion, and cheese. Combine eggs, mayonnaise, and milk. Pour egg mixture over pie shell. Bake at 350° for 50 to 60 minutes, or until knife comes out clean.
Yield: 4 servings

Arlene Zimmerman
Harrisburg, PA

WILD TURKEY PIE

3 tablespoons butter or margarine
¼ cup all-purpose flour
1¼ cups turkey or chicken broth
1 cup milk
2 cups cooked cubed wild turkey
1¼ cups canned small peas
½ cup sliced carrots
2 tablespoons chopped onion
1½ teaspoons salt
¼ teaspoon pepper
¼ teaspoon poultry seasoning
1 hard-cooked egg, sliced (optional)

FLAKY PASTRY

1 cup all-purpose flour
¾ teaspoon baking powder
½ teaspoon salt
⅓ cup shortening
3 tablespoons ice water

Melt butter in large heavy saucepan; blend in flour. Cook over low
heat until bubbly, stirring constantly. Gradually add broth and milk,
stirring constantly, and cook until thickened. Stir in turkey and next 7
ingredients. Heat. Spoon turkey mixture into a 1½-quart casserole.
Make pastry by combining flour with baking powder and salt. Cut in
shortening with a pastry blender until mixture resembles coarse meal.
Add ice water, little by little, until dough clings together when pressed
into a ball. Turn dough out onto a floured board, and roll to
¼ inch thickness. Place dough on top of casserole, pressing dough
firmly to fit rim. Cut slits in top of pastry. Bake at 400° for 30
minutes, or until golden brown.
Yield: 6 servings

Kris Gardner
Harpersville, AL

DEB'S TURKEY POT PIE

CRUST

1½ teaspoons salt
3 cups sifted all-purpose flour
1 cup butter-flavored shortening
½ cup ice water, as needed

FILLING

4 cups cooked diced turkey
¾ cup milk, divided
2 (10¾-ounce) cans cream of potato soup
2 (10¾-ounce) cans cream of mushroom soup
2 (15½-ounce) cans mixed vegetables, drained
1 (15-ounce) can green peas, drained
1 teaspoon pepper
1 teaspoon ground thyme

Mix salt into flour. Cut in shortening with a pastry blender until mixture resembles coarse meal. Sprinkle water over surface, 1 tablespoon at a time, and mix lightly with a fork, just until pastry holds together. Shape into a ball, divide in half, and roll out to ⅛ inch thick for bottom crust. Line crust in 10-inch pie pan. Bake at 425° for 10 to 12 minutes, or until lightly browned. For filling, combine turkey, ½ cup milk, and next 6 ingredients in large bowl. Pour filling into baked pie shell. Roll out remaining dough. Cover filling with top crust. Brush with remaining milk. Bake at 375° for 45 to 60 minutes until brown and bubbly.
Yield: 6 to 8 servings

Jim Arthur
Hixson, TN

SWEET POTATO TURKEY PIE

1 (29-ounce) can sweet potatoes, drained
2 tablespoons margarine, melted
¼ teaspoon pumpkin pie spice
Nonstick cooking spray
2 cups cooked cubed turkey
1 (10¾-ounce) low sodium cream of mushroom soup
1 (9-ounce) package frozen French-style green beans, thawed and
    drained
1 (2.8-ounce) can mushroom stems and pieces, drained
½ teaspoon salt
½ teaspoon pepper
2 tablespoons crushed canned fried onion rings

In medium bowl, blend sweet potatoes, margarine, and pumpkin pie
spice until smooth. Spray a 9-inch pie plate with nonstick cooking
spray. Line pie plate with sweet potato mixture to form shell. In
medium bowl, combine turkey and next 5 ingredients. Pour mixture
onto shell. Sprinkle with onion rings. Bake at 350° for 30 minutes, or
until hot and bubbly.
Serve with cranberry sauce.
Yield: 6 servings

National Turkey Federation
Reston, VA

RUSSELL'S TURKEY PIE WITH MUSHROOM SAUCE

⅓ cup chopped celery
6 tablespoons butter
⅔ cup water
1 (8-ounce) package herb-seasoned stuffing mix
3 eggs, beaten
1 (5-ounce) can evaporated milk
1 (single-serving) package dry mushroom soup mix
2 tablespoons chopped onion
2 tablespoons parsley
½ teaspoon pepper
1 teaspoon salt
3 cups chopped cooked turkey
Nonstick cooking spray
1 cup shredded Cheddar cheese

MUSHROOM SAUCE

2 (single-serving) packages dry mushroom soup mix
1 cup boiling water

Sauté celery in butter until tender. Add water and stuffing mix; set aside. Combine eggs, milk, 1 package soup mix, and next 4 ingredients. Stir in turkey. Coat a 10- or 12-inch skillet with nonstick cooking spray. Pour turkey mixture into skillet. Sprinkle with cheese. Top with stuffing mixture. Cover, and cook over medium heat for 10 to 15 minutes. To make sauce, dissolve mushroom soup mix and water. Serve mushroom sauce with pie.
Yield: 4 servings

Lee Russell
Mill Hall, PA

MOSTACCIOLI WITH SMOKED TURKEY AND ROASTED RED PEPPERS

Salt, as needed, divided
1 (16-ounce) package mostaccioli
½ cup turkey stock
6 tablespoons butter
8 ounces cooked smoked turkey, julienned
2 red peppers, roasted, peeled, seeded, julienned
Pepper, as needed
Crushed red pepper flakes
¾ cups grated Asiago cheese
2 tablespoons fresh basil, cut into strips

Bring a large pot of salted water to a boil. Add mostaccioli and cook al dente. Drain, and set aside. Heat stock in a saucepan; add mostaccioli, butter, and next 4 ingredients. Bring to a simmer, shaking pan occasionally to incorporate butter. Serve in warm bowls topped with cheese and basil.

Yield: 4 servings

Steve Zimmerman
H.K.'s Restaurant
The Lodge of The Four Seasons
Lake Ozark, MO

TURKEY CURRY

Nonstick cooking spray
1 cup chopped celery
½ cup chopped carrot
1 cup skim milk, divided
2 tablespoons cornstarch
¾ cup low-sodium chicken broth
2 tablespoons dried onion
½ teaspoon garlic powder
Curry powder, as needed
2 cups diced cooked turkey

Lightly coat a skillet with nonstick cooking spray. Sauté celery and carrot until tender. In a bowl, mix ¼ cup skim milk and cornstarch, stirring until smooth. Add broth and remaining milk, stirring until smooth. Pour sauce into skillet. Add onion, garlic powder, and 1 to 4 tablespoons curry powder, to taste. Cook over medium heat and stir 4 to 5 minutes, or until mixture thickens and bubbles. Add turkey. Cook and stir until turkey is heated through.
Serve over cooked rice, if desired.
Yield: 4 servings

Esther Burke
Kewaunee, WI

154

TURKEY HAWAIIAN

2 chicken-flavored bouillon cubes
¾ cup hot water
1 large onion, chopped
2 tablespoons vegetable oil
1 (9-ounce) package frozen sweet peas
1½ cups chopped celery
2 tablespoons cornstarch
1 tablespoon soy sauce
1 (14-ounce) can pineapple chunks, juice reserved
1 (4-ounce) can sliced mushrooms, juice reserved
1 (15-ounce) can sliced water chestnuts, drained
½ cup whole blanched almonds
3 cups julienned cooked turkey

Dissolve bouillon cubes in water. Sauté onion in oil until soft. Stir in peas and celery. Add chicken broth. Cover; simmer 5 minutes. Blend cornstarch and soy sauce until smooth; add pineapple and mushroom liquids. Stir cornstarch mixture into vegetables. Boil, stirring often, for 5 minutes, or until sauce thickens. Add pineapple, mushrooms, and remaining ingredients. Cover and simmer until hot.
Serve over hot cooked rice.
Yield: 4 to 6 servings

Shirley Grenoble
Altoona, PA

CROQUETTES

½ cup mayonnaise
½ teaspoon salt
2 tablespoons minced onion
⅛ teaspoon pepper
1 teaspoon Worcestershire sauce
1 tablespoon chopped parsley
2 tablespoons cold water
2 cups cooked chopped turkey
1 cup breadcrumbs
4 ounces saltines, finely crushed

Combine mayonnaise and next 5 ingredients. Add water, turkey, and breadcrumbs. Mix well. Let stand for 5 minutes. Shape into 6 to 7 croquettes, and roll in cracker crumbs. Bake at 450° at 15 to 20 minutes.
Yield: 4 servings

Lynn Boykin
Mobile, AL

MANNY'S PIZZA

CRUST

1 cup warm water
1 package yeast
1 teaspoon sugar
3 cups all-purpose flour, divided
2 teaspoons salt
3 tablespoons vegetable oil, divided

TOPPING

1 (8-ounce) can tomato sauce
¼ cup water
Garlic to taste
Oregano to taste
Salt to taste
Pepper to taste
12 ounces mozzarella cheese, shredded
1 pound cooked ground wild turkey
Shredded Parmesan cheese

In large bowl, combine water, yeast, and sugar. Add 1½ cups flour, salt, and 2 tablespoons oil. Mix thoroughly. Add remaining flour, and knead into firm ball. With paper towel, rub remaining oil throughout inside of bowl. Place dough in bowl. Cover; let rise 2 hours. Spread dough onto greased pizza pan. For topping, combine tomato sauce and next 5 ingredients. Spread over dough. Top with cheeses and turkey. Bake at 425° for 20 minutes.
Yield: 1 large or 2 small pizzas

Audrey Zimmerman
Alburtis, PA

TURKEY TURNOVERS

1 (15-ounce) package pie crusts
1 (10¾-ounce) can cream of chicken soup
½ cup plain yogurt
3 cups cooked cubed turkey
½ cup raisins or dried currants
¼ cup chopped peanuts
¼ cup shredded coconut
¼ cup chopped green onions
1 teaspoon curry powder
1 egg yolk
1 teaspoon water

Let pie crusts stand at room temperature for 15 to 20 minutes. In medium bowl, combine soup and yogurt. Mix in turkey, and next 5 ingredients. Unfold crusts. Place on ungreased cookie sheet, and press fold lines. Spoon half of turkey mixture onto half of crust. Fold crust over; pinch and seal edges. Cut slits in top of crust. Repeat with remaining crust and turkey mixture. In small bowl, beat egg yolk with water. Brush over tops of crusts. Bake at 375° for 30 to 40 minutes, or until deep golden brown. Cut each turnover into quarters.
Yield: 6 to 8 servings

Nick Crafton
Memphis, TN

VIKING TURKEY BURGERS

1 pound ground turkey breast
1½ tablespoons prepared horseradish
1½ teaspoons Dijon-style mustard
1½ teaspoons paprika
¼ teaspoon pepper
⅛ teaspoon salt
Nonstick cooking spray
4 hamburger buns, toasted

In large bowl, combine turkey and next 5 ingredients. Shape meat into four, ½-inch-thick patties. Lightly coat broiler pan with nonstick cooking spray. Broil, about 6 inches from heat, for 3 to 4 minutes per side, or until no longer pink in center. Serve on buns.
Yield: 4 servings

National Turkey Federation
Reston, VA

H. K.'S TURKEY BURGER

¾ cup heavy cream
4 eggs
½ bunch parsley, chopped
½ cup chopped fresh thyme
½ cup chopped fresh chives
2 pounds mushrooms, destemmed, sliced
2 tablespoons chopped garlic
1 small onion, diced
2 tablespoons vegetable oil
5 pounds ground turkey
Salt to taste
Pepper to taste
1¼ cups fine breadcrumbs

Mix cream and next 4 ingredients. Cover and refrigerate. Sauté
mushroom, garlic, and onion in oil until tender; add to cream
mixture. Transfer to mixer; add turkey, salt, and pepper, and mix until
incorporated. Slowly add breadcrumbs; don't over mix. Divide into 7-
ounce patties. Grill or pan fry until desired degree of doneness.
Yield: 15 servings

Steve Zimmerman
H.K.'s Restaurant
The Lodge of The Four Seasons
Lake Ozark, MO

REUBEN TURKEY BURGERS

1 Recipe Turkey Burger Plus (recipe follows)
4 ounces Swiss cheese
4 hamburger buns, toasted
4 tablespoons sauerkraut, drained and rinsed, divided
4 tablespoons Thousand Island or Russian dressing, divided

Prepare Basic Burgers according to recipe. During last minute of
broiling, top each burger with cheese. Once melted, place burgers on
buns, and top each with 1 tablespoon sauerkraut and 1 tablespoon
Russian dressing. Heat, if desired.
Yield: 4 servings

National Turkey Federation
Reston, VA

TURKEY BURGER PLUS

1 pound ground turkey breast
½ cup seasoned breadcrumbs
⅓ cup diced onion
1 egg, beaten
1 teaspoon soy sauce
1 teaspoon Worcestershire sauce
½ teaspoon garlic powder
¼ teaspoon dry mustard
Nonstick cooking spray
4 hamburger buns, toasted

In large bowl, combine turkey and next 7 ingredients. Shape meat into four, ½-inch-thick patties. Coat broiler pan with nonstick cooking spray. Broil about 6 inches from heat, 3 to 4 minutes per side, or until no longer pink in center. Serve on buns.
Yield: 4 servings

National Turkey Federation
Reston, VA

TURKEY BURGERS AL GRECO

1 Recipe Turkey Burger Plus (recipe above)
4 mini pitas
6 tablespoons feta cheese, crumbled
1 cup chopped tomato
½ cup thinly sliced cucumber
½ cup thinly sliced onion

Prepare Basic Burgers according to recipe. To open pitas, cut off tops: insert burgers. Evenly sprinkle cheese and remaining ingredients onto each burger.
Yield: 4 servings

National Turkey Federation
Reston, VA

MEXICAN-TOPPED TURKEY BURGERS

1 Recipe Turkey Burger Plus (recipe on previous page)
4 ounces Monterey Jack cheese, divided
½ cup imitation sour cream
¼ cup chunky salsa
½ teaspoon chopped fresh cilantro
4 hamburger buns, toasted
1 avocado, sliced (optional)

Prepare Basic Burgers according to recipe. Top each burger with cheese, and broil until melted. In small bowl, combine sour cream, salsa, and cilantro. Serve burgers on buns topped with sauce and avocado, if desired.
Yield: 4 servings

National Turkey Federation
Reston, VA

CREAMY MUSHROOM TURKEY BURGERS

1 Recipe Turkey Burger Plus (recipe on previous page)
2 tablespoons margarine
¼ teaspoon dried thyme leaves
½ pound mushrooms, thinly sliced
2 tablespoons brandy
½ teaspoon garlic powder
⅛ teaspoon salt
⅛ teaspoon pepper
1 cup plain low-fat yogurt

Prepare Basic Burgers according to recipe. In medium skillet over medium-high heat, melt margarine, add thyme, and sauté mushroom for 1 to 2 minutes. Add brandy, and next 3 ingredients; cook for 1 minute. Stir in yogurt, and heat until warm. Serve burger topped with mushroom sauce.
Yield: 4 servings

National Turkey Federation
Reston, VA

THREE-CHEESE BISTRO TURKEY BURGERS

1½ pounds ground turkey breast
¼ cup chopped mango chutney
¼ cup Parmesan cheese
¼ cup seasoned breadcrumbs
3 tablespoons minced parsley
2 tablespoons chopped walnuts
Salt to taste
Pepper to taste
2 ounces cream cheese, softened
2 ounces Gorgonzola or blue cheese, crumbled
4 (1-inch-thick) slices sourdough French bread
2 teaspoons olive oil
1 medium tomato, sliced
1 small onion, sliced
4 teaspoons grainy Dijon-style mustard

Prepare grill for direct-heat cooking. In medium bowl, combine turkey and next 7 ingredients. Divide into 8 patties, approximately 4½ inches in diameter. In small bowl, combine cheeses. Divide cheese mixture into 4 balls; flatten slightly. Place balls in center of patties; top with remaining patties. Pinch edges together to seal. Grill over medium-high heat 4 to 6 minutes. Turn, and cook, covered, 6 to 8 minutes, or until meat thermometer registers 160° to 165°, and meat is no longer pink. Brush both sides of bread with olive oil. Toast bread on both sides. To serve, place burgers on bread, and top with tomato, onion, and mustard.
Yield: 4 servings

National Turkey Federation
Reston, VA

RUMANIAN TURKEY BURGERS

1 pound ground turkey breast
1 to 2 cloves garlic, crushed
½ teaspoons dried thyme
½ teaspoon salt
¼ teaspoon allspice
¼ teaspoon ground cloves
¼ teaspoon pepper
Nonstick cooking spray
4 hamburger buns, toasted

In large bowl, combine turkey and next 6 ingredients. Shape into 4 patties, ½-inch thick. Lightly coat broiler pan with nonstick cooking spray. Broil, about 6 inches from heat, 3 to 4 minutes per side, or until no longer pink in center. Serve on buns.
Yield: 4 servings

National Turkey Federation
Reston, VA

TURKEY-TOMATO MEATBALLS

8 to 10 sun-dried tomatoes
1 cup boiling water
3 pounds ground turkey breast
1 tablespoon fennel seed
1 tablespoon minced garlic
1 tablespoon salt
½ teaspoon pepper
Nonstick cooking spray

In small bowl, soak tomatoes in water, 2 to 5 minutes, or until soft. Drain, reserving ½ cup liquid. Chop tomatoes. In large bowl, combine tomato, reserved liquid, turkey, and next 4 ingredients. Cover, and refrigerate 8 hours or overnight. Form into 1-inch meatballs. Coat two 15x10x2-inch baking pans with nonstick cooking spray. Bake at 400° for 15 to 20 minutes, or until no longer pink in center.
Yield: 30 meatballs

National Turkey Federation
Reston, VA

HICKORY-SMOKED TURKEY SPREAD

2 cups chopped hickory-smoked turkey
1 cup finely chopped pecans
½ cup mayonnaise
½ cup finely chopped celery
Minced garlic, as needed

Combine all ingredients. Use as a sandwich spread.
Yield: 4 to 6 servings

Teresa Bates
Bates House of Turkey
Fort Deposit, AL

TURKEY ASPARAGUS MELT

¼ cup mayonnaise or light sour cream
2 tablespoons Dijon mustard
½ teaspoon dried sage leaves, crushed
3 (6-inch-long) sourdough hoagie buns, split lengthwise
12 ounces sliced cooked turkey
1 (15-ounce) can asparagus spears, drained
½ cup red onion, cut into rings
1½ cups shredded colby, Monterey Jack, or Cheddar cheese

In small bowl, combine mayonnaise, mustard, and sage. Mix well.
Spread 1 to 2 tablespoons mixture on each bun bottom. Layer with
turkey, asparagus, onion, and cheese. Broil sandwiches 4 to 6 inches
from heat for 3 to 4 minutes, until thoroughly heated and cheese is
bubbly. Replace top bun half.
Yield: 6 servings

Mike Halter
East Ridge, TN

163

MEXICAN FIESTA TURKEY WINGS

2 pounds turkey wings
1 (15-ounce) can chunky tomato sauce
1 (1¼-ounce) package taco seasoning mix
1 cup shredded Cheddar cheese

Boil turkey wings in water to cover. Lower heat and cover; simmer 2 hours. Discard turkey broth. Mix tomato sauce and taco mix. Pour over turkey. Simmer, covered, for 15 minutes. Uncover; sprinkle with cheese. Cover; heat 3 to 5 minutes, until cheese melts.
Yield: 2 servings

Missouri Poultry Federation
Columbia, MO

SPICY ROAST TURKEY WINGS

6 turkey wings
Water, as needed
Salt, as needed
¼ teaspoon cinnamon
¼ teaspoon nutmeg
¼ teaspoon allspice
¼ teaspoon pepper

Place turkey wings in large saucepan. Add enough water to cover. Add salt. Cover with lid. Cook over moderate heat until tender, about 40 minutes. Cool slightly. Reserve broth. Remove wings, and rub well with cinnamon and remaining ingredients. Place wings in roasting pan. Roast at 350°, basting frequently with broth and pan drippings, for 30 minutes or until golden brown.
Yield: 6 servings

Lynn Boykin
Mobile, AL

FRIED TURKEY NUGGETS

1 pound white cornmeal
4 ounces seasoned salt
2 tablespoons black or cayenne pepper
2 tablespoons onion salt
4 pounds boneless turkey, cubed
Vegetable oil

Combine cornmeal with next 3 ingredients. Roll turkey in cornmeal mixture. Heat oil to 350° and deep fry 2 minutes.
Yield: 8 to 10 servings

Mike Chlebowski
Beaver Dam, WI

GEORGE'S WILD TURKEY JERKY

1 pound boneless turkey
1 teaspoon salt
¼ teaspoon pepper
1 teaspoon garlic powder
2 tablespoons Worcestershire sauce
2 tablespoons liquid smoke

Cut turkey into strips. Mix salt and remaining ingredients in a medium bowl. Combine turkey with marinade. Cover, and refrigerate for 6 to 12 hours. Cover oven rack with foil. Place turkey on foil. Bake at 160° for 4 hours. Turn, and bake another 4 hours.
Yield: 4 servings

Dwane George
Cheyenne, WY

GRILLED TURKEY LEGS

2 turkey drumsticks
2 turkey thighs
1 (24-ounce) bottle Italian dressing

Marinate turkey in dressing at least 12 hours, or overnight. Grill turkey about 40 minutes, brushing often with marinade, or until done. **Yield**: 4 servings

Mike Halter
East Ridge, TN

TURKEY LEG YUM-YUMS

2 whole wild turkey legs
Salt, as needed
Pepper, as needed
1 cup milk
1½ cups self-rising flour or biscuit mix
1 tablespoon soft margarine
Vegetable oil, as needed

Boil turkey legs until tender. Cool. Slice meat into 1-inch strips. Season with salt and pepper. Combine milk, and next 2 ingredients to make a stiff batter. Dip strips in batter. Heat oil in skillet, and fry, turning once. Drain on paper towels. **Yield**: 4 servings

Leola Smith
Edgefield, SC

WILD TURKEY CHILI

3 pounds ground wild turkey
2 cups chopped celery
6 medium onions, chopped
2 cloves garlic
½ teaspoon cayenne pepper
1 teaspoon marjoram
1 teaspoon cumin
3 teaspoons salt
2 (16-ounce) can diced tomatoes
½ cup chili powder
1 tablespoon paprika
4 cups tomato juice
2 (20-ounce) cans pinto beans, undrained

In large stockpot, brown turkey. Add celery, and next 10 ingredients in order listed. Simmer for 60 minutes. Add pinto beans, and simmer an additional 60 minutes.
Yield: 8 to 10 servings

Jim Arthur
Hixson, TN

EASY TURKEY CHILI

2 tablespoons oil
2 pounds ground turkey
½ cup chopped onion
2 cloves garlic, minced
2 tablespoons chili powder (or to taste)
1 tablespoon paprika
2 teaspoons cumin
1 teaspoon salt
Freshly ground pepper, to taste
1 (28-ounce) can crushed tomatoes
2 (15-ounce) cans red kidney beans, drained

Heat oil in a large skillet over medium heat. Add turkey and onion. Cook, and stir about 4 to 5 minutes, or until turkey is no longer pink. Stir in garlic and next 6 ingredients. Cover. Over high heat, bring to a boil. Reduce heat, and simmer for 1 hour. Add beans; cook until heated throughout.
May be prepared a day ahead. Simmer 1 hour before serving.
Yield: 8 servings

Missouri Poultry Federation
Columbia, MO

167

I'm a professional fisherman. My great love of turkey hunting defies reason. For three months of the year, I am compelled to be up early and out in the spring woods. I think it's the gobble that gets me going. There's just no sound like it. So I put my career on temporary hold and, at great cost, sometimes with impossible schedules and with absolutely nothing to gain other than the joy of turkey hunting, I hit the trail. I guess it's much like being a chocoholic or a fishoholic. I'm a turkoholic, too, and each spring I can hardly wait to indulge myself.

Roland Martin
Professional Fisherman and
Outdoor TV Personality
Clewiston, FL

TURKEY CROQUETTES

2 cups cooked ground or finely chopped turkey
1 (10¾-ounce) can cream of mushroom soup
1 egg
2 tablespoons chopped onion
20 saltine crackers, finely crushed
Vegetable oil

Mix first 4 ingredients. Shape into patties, roll in cracker crumbs, and brown in a large skillet in 1-inch vegetable oil.
Yield: 4 to 6 servings

LETS GIVE THANKS

Thanksgiving Menus from Region to Region

Peter Ruiz © 1995

A man's responsibility to his family can many times be met just by being in our forests and fields as the quiet dawn breaks, listening to wild turkeys gobbling, or waiting for that great white-tailed buck to appear. I know such experiences relieve stress, and I believe they may help prolong life.

Ron Fretts
Scottdale, PA

MID-ATLANTIC REGIONAL THANKSGIVING

We came from a part of Pennsylvania that has a rich German Mennonite (Pennsylvania Dutch) heritage, known for good country cooking. These recipes are a part of that heritage and a typical Thanksgiving at our home.

Often on Thanksgiving morning there will be hunting for wild turkeys, rabbits, and pheasants. Later, back at home, after giving thanks for our many blessings, the whole family enjoys good food and good company.

Ron and Pat Fretts

MENU

Roasted Wild Turkey*
Stuffing*
Giblet Gravy* (see page 175)
Mashed Potatoes
Candied Sweet Potatoes*
Green Beans with Ham*
Cranberry Salad*
Fruit Salad
Apple-Walnut Upside-Down Pie*
Traditional Pumpkin Pie* (see page 176)

*recipe included

ROASTED WILD TURKEY

1 (12-pound) wild turkey
Salt to taste

STUFFING

2 loaves day-old bread, cubed
1 cup chopped onion
1 cup chopped celery
2 sticks butter, melted
2 eggs
Pepper to taste
Poultry seasoning to taste
Turkey broth

Rinse turkey in cold water. Rub inside and outside of bird with salt. To make stuffing, combine bread and next 6 ingredients. Moisten with broth to desired texture. Stuff turkey. Roast turkey at 350° for about 3½ hours.
Yield: 10 to 12 servings

CANDIED SWEET POTATOES

½ cup packed brown sugar
½ stick margarine
1 (29-ounce) can sweet potatoes, liquid reserved
2 cups marshmallows
½ cup chopped nuts, optional

Boil the reserved liquid with brown sugar and margarine until thickened. Add sweet potatoes, cover, and bake at 350° for 1 hour. In the last 10 minutes, add marshmallows and nuts.
Yield: 6 servings

GREEN BEANS WITH HAM

2 cups cooked cubed ham
1 small onion, diced
3 (16-ounce) cans green beans, liquid reserved
Salt to taste
Pepper to taste

In a large skillet, brown ham slowly over low heat. Add onion, and continue cooking until brown. Remove ham and onion from pan. Pour green bean liquid into pan; cook down. Stir in beans, ham, and onion. Add salt and pepper to taste. Cook until mixture is warm.
Yield: 8 to 10 servings

CRANBERRY SALAD

½ pound cranberries, washed
2 oranges, washed, stemmed, seeded, quartered
3 apples, cored, pared, and finely chopped
¼ cup chopped walnuts
1½ cups sugar
1 (3-ounce) package cherry or strawberry gelatin
1 cup hot water
1 cup cold water

Grind cranberries and oranges in food processor. Mix in apples, nuts, and sugar. Dissolve gelatin in hot water. Add cold water. When gelatin mixture cools, add fruit, pour into mold; refrigerate to set.
Yield: 6 servings

APPLE-WALNUT UPSIDE DOWN PIE

⅓ cup brown sugar
¼ cup melted butter
¼ cup chopped walnuts
Pastry for 2-crust pie
3½ cups sliced apples, peeled
¾ cup sugar
1 teaspoon cinnamon
Dash of nutmeg
Dash of salt

Butter a 9-inch pie pan. Sprinkle with brown sugar. Pour melted butter over sugar, and stir. Sprinkle nuts onto pan. Roll out pastry for bottom crust; place atop nuts. Top pastry with apples. In small bowl, mix sugar and remaining ingredients; sprinkle over apples. Fit top crust over apples; trim, seal, and crimp edges. Prick top crust with fork. Bake at 350° for 45 minutes, or until crust is lightly browned. Turn onto plate immediately.
Yield: 8 servings

WESTERN REGIONAL THANKSGIVING

When the West was pioneered, times were hard. Long days in the wagons on the Oregon Trail was a harsh way of life. The heat of the plains and deserts, the bitter cold and snow of the Rockies and Cascade Mountains became common occurrences to the settlers. Thanksgiving Day marked a time of joy and celebration. The settlers were thankful for a break in or an end to the long journey.

In these modern times folks in the West celebrate Thanksgiving Day for basically the same reasons. The families are thankful for togetherness and another wonderful year of life in America.

Mike Carey
Tumalo, OR

MENU

Paper-Wrapped Roast Wild Turkey*
Oyster Stuffing*
Giblet Gravy*
Ambrosia Salad*
Rich Mashed Potatoes*
Cauliflower with Cheese Sauce*
Cranberry Sauce
Home-baked Bread
Traditional Pumpkin Pie*

Recipe Included

PAPER-WRAPPED ROAST WILD TURKEY

1 (16-pound) wild turkey
½ stick butter, chilled and cut into chips
Thickly sliced bacon
1 cup turkey stock
1½ cups red wine

Rinse turkey in cold water. Fill with Oyster Stuffing. Truss legs. Make small slits in skin over breasts and thighs. Insert butter chips. Place turkey breast side down in roasting pan. Lay bacon over back and sides of turkey. Cover completely with thick paper towels. Mix stock and wine. Pour over towels. Do not tent with foil. Bake at 350° for 4 hours, basting constantly. Thirty minutes before turkey is done, remove towels.
Yield: 16 to 20 servings

OYSTER STUFFING

2 cups all-purpose flour
½ cup sugar
8 teaspoons baking powder
1½ teaspoons salt
2 cups yellow cornmeal
2 eggs
2 cups milk
½ cup vegetable oil
1 pint oysters, lightly sautéed in 1 tablespoon butter

Sift flour with next 4 ingredients. Beat eggs; then add milk, oil, and oysters. Add this mixture to dry ingredients, and mix until moistened. Stuff turkey with mixture or place oyster stuffing in two buttered 9x9x2-inch square pans. Bake at 425° degrees for 30 to 40 minutes.
Yield: stuffing for one large turkey or about 16 servings.

GIBLET GRAVY

1 turkey heart
1 turkey neck
1 turkey gizzard
3 stalks celery
½ small onion, sliced
Salt to taste
Pepper to taste
⅓ cup all-purpose flour
1 cup water

Place heart and next 4 ingredients in a large saucepan. Cover with water. Add salt and pepper. Bring to a boil; reduce heat, and simmer, covered, for 45 minutes or until tender. Strain, reserving stock. Chop meat. Cook stock and meat in a skillet over moderate heat. In a jar, shake flour and water until well blended. Add to stock until it reaches desired thickness.
Yield: 2 cups

AMBROSIA SALAD

3 apples, peeled, cored, cubed
2 (11-ounce) cans mandarin oranges, drained
½ cup chopped walnuts
Raisins, optional
½ cup shredded coconut
½ cup mayonnaise
Sugar to taste

Place first 5 ingredients in a bowl. Add mayonnaise; mix well. Add sugar, to taste.
Yield: 4 to 6 servings

CAULIFLOWER WITH CHEESE SAUCE

1 head cauliflower
8 ounces Cheddar cheese, shredded
1½ cups milk

Steam cauliflower until tender. Heat milk and cheese in double boiler. Top cauliflower with cheese sauce.
Yield: 4 to 6 servings

175

RICH MASHED POTATOES

8 medium potatoes
½ cup mayonnaise
½ cup Parmesan cheese
⅓ cup margarine
Splash of milk
Salt to taste
Pepper to taste

Peel and quarter potatoes. Place in large saucepan, cover with water, and boil until almost tender. Strain potatoes, add remaining ingredients, and mash.
Yield: 4 servings

TRADITIONAL PUMPKIN PIE

1½ cups sugar
¾ cup all-purpose flour
3 teaspoons cinnamon
½ teaspoon allspice
½ teaspoon nutmeg
¼ teaspoon ginger
1 teaspoon salt
1 (29-ounce) can pure pumpkin
6 eggs, separated
3 cups evaporated milk
3 cups hot water
1 tablespoon vanilla
4 to 5 (9-inch) pie shells

Mix sugar and next 6 ingredients in a large bowl. Mix in pumpkin. Beat egg yolks until thick and light-colored. Combine with pumpkin mixture. Mix in milk, water, and vanilla. Beat egg whites until soft peaks form; fold into pumpkin mixture. Divide pumpkin mixture among pie shells. Bake at 425° for 20 minutes; reduce heat to 375° and bake until lightly browned and no longer watery, about 35 to 45 minutes.
Yield: 32 to 40 servings

MIDWESTERN REGIONAL THANKSGIVING

Out here in the Midwest, we have been very blessed. Each year is like a "Walton's" Thanksgiving, with grandchildren standing on chairs to help make some of the goodies. As a farming region, we are especially thankful for our harvest, family, and homes. Thanksgiving Day is when we eat from the land and gather our family under one roof to give thanks for all that we have and all that we are.

Patsy Murphy
Williamstown, MO

MENU

Stuffed Midwestern Wild Turkey* (see page 112)
Giblet Gravy* (see page 175)
Bread Dressing*
Homemade Noodles
Scalloped Corn*
Candied Sweet Potatoes* (see page 171)
Sweet Rolls*
Midwest Pumpkin Pie*

*recipe included

BREAD DRESSING

2 sticks butter
¾ finely minced onion
1½ cups chopped celery
12 cups coarse breadcrumbs made from day-old homemade bread
1 tablespoon salt
1 tablespoon pepper
¼ teaspoon sage
½ teaspoon poultry seasoning
Hot water or turkey broth
1 egg, beaten
Nonstick cooking spray

Melt butter in large, heavy skillet. Add onion and celery; cook until onion is clear. Add enough breadcrumbs to absorb onion mixture. Transfer to a large bowl. Mix in remaining breadcrumbs and next 4 ingredients. Stir in hot water or broth to moisten. Incorporate egg. Coat a 13x9x2-inch baking dish with nonstick cooking spray. Add mixture and bake at 350° until dressing turns light brown.
Yield: 8 to 10 servings

SCALLOPED CORN

1 (10¾-ounce) can cream of celery soup
¾ cup milk
Pepper to taste
2 to 3 cups canned kernel corn or fresh corn, cut off the cob
1 small onion, diced
1 tablespoon butter

Blend soup, milk, and pepper. In a 1½-quart casserole, layer corn, onion, and soup mixture. Dot with butter. Cover, and bake at 375° for 1 hour. Uncover, and bake 15 minutes.
May be baked ahead and reheated.
Yield: 4 servings

SWEET ROLLS

¾ cup milk
½ stick butter, softened
¼ cup warm water
3½ cups all-purpose flour, divided
1 teaspoon salt
¼ cup sugar
1 (¼-ounce) package dry yeast
1 egg

Scald milk; pour into large mixing bowl. Add butter and water . Combine 1¾ cups flour, salt, sugar, and yeast; add to milk mixture, and beat 2 minutes. Add egg. Beat 1 minute. Stir in remaining flour until thick. Knead a few minutes. Let rise until doubled in bulk, about 2½ hours. Roll into small balls a little smaller than baseballs. Transfer dough balls to pans, and let rise until doubled in size, about 1 hour. Bake at 375° for 15 to 20 minutes.
Yield: 2 to 3 dozen

MIDWEST PUMPKIN PIE

3 eggs
1 cup pumpkin
1 cup milk
1 tablespoon butter
1 teaspoon pumpkin pie spice
½ cup sugar
Pinch of salt
1 (9-inch) pie shell

Beat eggs and next 2 ingredients. Add butter, and next 3 ingredients. Mix thoroughly. Pour into pie shell, and bake at 350° for 10 minutes; reduce heat, and bake 30 to 35 minutes until a knife inserted between center and rim comes out clean.
Yield: 4 to 6 servings

SOUTHWESTERN REGIONAL THANKSGIVING

The proximity of the Southwestern states to the border with Mexico and its Spanish influences, combined with early American pioneer grit, makes for a Thanksgiving fare ranging from salsa to squash. Add to this mix the region's long and deep Native American history, which includes the exploits of Geronimo and Cochise, and the area's abundance of wildlife (javelina, elk, wild turkey, and deer), and the Southwestern Thanksgiving becomes one steeped in history and diversity. There is not one particular way to characterize Thanksgiving in the Southwest. Each family gives thanks the way their ancestors have done for generations.

Rick Fields
Tucson, AZ

MENU

Field's Fantasy Pistachio Salad*
Stuffed Roasted Wild Turkey*
Giblet Gravy* (see page 175)
Calabaoitas Con Queso*
Classic Green Bean Casserole*
Pecan Pie*

*recipe included

FIELD'S FANTASY PISTACHIO SALAD

1 (8-ounce) can crushed pineapple
1 (3-ounce) box pistachio-flavored instant pudding mix
1 (16-ounce) container frozen whipped topping, thawed slightly
½ cup coarsely chopped pecans
2 tablespoons coconut
2 cups miniature marshmallows
Maraschino cherries

In large bowl, blend pineapple with pudding mix. Add frozen whipped topping, and mix thoroughly. Add pecans, coconut, and marshmallows. Garnish with cherries.
Yield: 6 to 8 servings

STUFFED ROASTED WILD TURKEY

2 sticks butter, divided
1 cup finely chopped shallots or scallions
5 cups fresh breadcrumbs
2 teaspoons salt
1 cup finely chopped parsley
1 cup pistachio nuts or pine nuts
1 teaspoon freshly ground black pepper
1 (12-pound) wild turkey
Salt to taste
Pepper to taste

BASTING SOLUTION

Melted butter
White wine

Melt 1 stick butter in a skillet. Sauté shallot until limp. Thoroughly mix in breadcrumbs, and next 4 ingredients. Add more melted butter if stuffing seems too dry. Stuff turkey loosely. Truss. Rub skin with remaining butter, salt, and pepper. Make basting solution of equal parts of melted butter and white wine. Roast turkey on a rack at 325° for 22 to 25 minutes per pound, basting often.
Serve with giblet gravy and a robust red wine.
Yield: 10 to 12 servings

CALABAOITAS CON QUESO

6 medium summer squash (yellow or zucchini), cubed
1 onion, minced
2 tomatoes, peeled and chopped
1 tablespoon olive oil
2 cups shredded queso fresco or processed cheese loaf
Salt to taste
Pepper to taste

Combine the squash, onion, tomatoes, and olive oil in a saucepan; cover and cook for 20 minutes. Remove cover, add cheese, salt, and pepper, and cook 5 minutes longer, stirring constantly.
Yield: 4 to 8 servings

181

CLASSIC GREEN BEAN CASSEROLE

1 (10¾-ounce) can cream of mushroom soup
½ cup milk
1 teaspoon soy sauce
Dash of pepper
2 (14.5-ounce) can green beans, any style, drained
1 (2.8-ounce) can fried onion rings, divided

In a 1½-quart casserole, combine soup and next 3 ingredients. Stir in green beans, and a half can of onion rings. Bake at 350° for 25 minutes; stir. Top with remaining onions. Bake 5 minutes longer.
Yield: 4 to 6 servings

PECAN PIE

5 eggs
1 cup sugar
1 cup light or dark corn syrup
2 tablespoons margarine, melted
1 teaspoon vanilla
1½ cups pecan halves
1 (9-inch) pie shell

In a medium bowl, beat eggs lightly. Add sugar and next 3 ingredients. Stir until well blended. Place pecans on bottom of pie shell. Pour egg mixture atop pecans. Bake at 350° for 50 to 55 minutes, or until knife inserted into center of pie comes out clean.
Yield: 8 servings

NORTHEASTERN REGIONAL THANKSGIVING

Thanksgiving in the Northeast is a special time to give thanks for the bounty of the land and to share time and stories with friends and family. Thanksgiving is also a day of sporting activities. Traditionally, an early-morning breakfast is followed by spending the morning in the cold crisp woods in search of the white-tailed deer. Sitting in the cold, sometimes snow-covered woods and swamps waiting for the sight or sound of old mossy horn is an important part of Thanksgiving in the Northeast. About noon everyone gathers at the traditional table to give thanks for family, friends, and the bounty produced by the spoils of the land.

Tom Nannery
Durham, ME

MENU

Charcoal-Grilled Wild Turkey* (page 123) or
Baked Turkey* (page 108)
Country-Style Stuffing*
Creamed Onions*
Mashed Butternut Squash
Harvard Beets*
Cranberry-Nut Bread
Blueberry Pie*

recipe included

COUNTRY-STYLE STUFFING

2 cups water
1 stick butter
2 (16-ounce) bags herb-seasoned cubed stuffing mix
2 cups sautéed chopped mushrooms
1 cup sautéed chopped celery
1 cup sautéed chopped onions
1 cup chopped cooked turkey giblets
2 cups chopped cranberries

Heat water and butter to a boil. Remove from heat, and add stuffing, tossing lightly until moist throughout. Add mushrooms, and remaining ingredients, mixing thoroughly. Stuff wild turkey before roasting.
Yield: enough stuffing for an 18 to 20 pound turkey

CREAMED ONIONS

2 pounds small white onions, peeled
2 tablespoons butter
2 tablespoons all-purpose flour
½ teaspoon salt
⅛ teaspoon freshly ground pepper
1½ cups half-and-half
Breadcrumbs

Boil onions until tender, about 15 to 18 minutes. Drain. Transfer to casserole. Melt butter in large saucepan over low heat. Blend in flour, salt, and pepper. Cook, stirring constantly, until mixture is smooth and bubbly. Stir in half-and-half. Heat to boiling, stirring constantly for 1 minute. Pour sauce over onions. Sprinkle with breadcrumbs. Bake, uncovered, at 325° for 30 minutes.
Yield: 8 to 10 servings

184

HARVARD BEETS

5 medium beets, unpeeled
1 tablespoon cornstarch
1 tablespoon sugar
¼ teaspoon salt
Pinch of pepper
⅔ cup water
¼ cup vinegar

Cover beets with water. Simmer 35 to 45 minutes, or until tender.
Drain and cool. Peel; cut into ¼-inch slices. In small saucepan, mix
cornstarch and next 3 ingredients. Stir in water and vinegar. Cook,
stirring constantly, until mixture boils and thickens. Boil and stir for 1
minute more. Stir in beets, and heat thoroughly.
Yield: 4 servings

BLUEBERRY PIE

4 cups blueberries, divided
1 (9-inch) pie shell, baked
3 tablespoons cornstarch
1 cup sugar
¼ teaspoon salt
½ teaspoon cinnamon
½ cup water
1 tablespoon butter
½ cup whipping cream, whipped

Spread 1 cup blueberries into pie shell. In medium saucepan over low
heat, mix cornstarch and next 4 ingredients. Cook, stirring constantly,
until mixture thickens. Stir in butter. Remove from heat. Cool. Add 3
cups blueberries to sauce, and pour into pie shell. Chill. Top with
whipped cream.
Yield: 8 servings

TEXAS/OKLAHOMA REGIONAL THANKSGIVING

The Indians of Oklahoma hunted the wild turkey long before the early settlers came to their land. They possessed not only the skills to harvest these magnificent birds, but also a spiritual appreciation for what the gods had given them.

As early settlers moved into the regions of Oklahoma and Texas, farms and ranches became a way of life. As in many areas of the United States, the early settlers lived off the land. The small garden plots out back provided the vegetables for those Thanksgiving meals. The native pecans, which were abundant along the rivers and bottom lands, provided the nuts for many delicious pies and other desserts.

Even with a Western flair, Thanksgiving Day is—and always will be—that special day when we all give thanks to our Creator for the life he has given us.

Jim Lillis
Sherman, TX

MENU

Foil-Wrapped Roast Turkey*
Giblet Gravy* (see page 175)
Cornbread Dressing* (see page 71)
Cranberry Sauce*
Congealed Salad
Carrot and Cucumber Salad
Candied Sweets*
Classic Green Bean Casserole* (see page 182)
Southern Pecan Pie*
Amaretto Grapes*

recipe included

186

FOIL-WRAPPED ROAST TURKEY

1 (12-pound) turkey
Salt to taste
Pepper to taste
Butter
Turkey giblets

Rinse turkey in cold water. Dry thoroughly. Rub cavity with salt and pepper. Rub skin with butter. Place giblets inside cavity. Wrap turkey in foil. Place turkey, breast side up, in bottom of shallow roasting pan. Roast at 450° for 2¾ to 3 hours.
Yield: 14 to 16 servings

CRANBERRY SAUCE

2 (1-pound) bags cranberries, washed
3 cups sugar

Boil cranberries in enough water to cover until berries pop. Add sugar, and boil slowly until mixture thickens. Cool. Refrigerate for 8 hours or overnight.
Yield: 6 to 8 servings

CANDIED SWEETS

4 to 5 sweet potatoes, peeled and quartered
2 cups sugar
¾ cup water
1 teaspoon cinnamon
¼ teaspoon salt
2 tablespoons vinegar
4 tablespoons butter

Boil potatoes until tender. Drain. In small saucepan, boil remaining ingredients for 5 minutes. Pour sauce over potatoes. Bake in 2-quart casserole dish at 350° for 1 hour.
Yield: 4 to 6 servings

SOUTHERN PECAN PIE

3 eggs
⅔ cup sugar
Dash salt
1 cup dark corn syrup
½ cup melted butter or margarine
1 cup pecan halves
1 (9-inch) unbaked pie shell

Beat eggs thoroughly with sugar, salt, corn syrup, and melted butter. Add pecans; then pour mixture into pie shell. Bake at 350° for 50 minutes or until knife, inserted halfway between outside edge and center of filling, comes out clean. Cool before serving.

AMARETTO GRAPES

2 (8-ounce) packages cream cheese, softened
½ cup sugar
¼ cup Amaretto
2½ pounds red seedless grapes

Blend cream cheese with sugar and Amaretto until smooth and creamy. Gently stir in grapes. Refrigerate at least 4 hours before serving.
Yield: 6 to 8 servings

SOUTHERN REGIONAL
THANKSGIVING

The South is known for its "Southern Tradition," and on Thanksgiving Day this is more evident than at other times during the year. In the South, a certain reverenced pride is passed from one generation to the next for God, country, and family. In many homes across the South, Thanksgiving is the day that mothers share the kitchen with their daughters, cooking a meal just as their grandmothers had done before, while fathers and sons enjoy the outdoors, hunting together or passing a football just as their grandfathers before them.

A traditional Thanksgiving table in the South is circled by the family, and often each one takes a turn in giving thanks to God for the abundant life that we are granted. From the youngest child's thanks for the little flowers to the great-grandparent's thanks for an abundant life, Thanksgiving Day is one that Southern families are united as one people, under one God, and in this great country, America. For these reasons we give thanks.

Nancy DeLoach
Saluda, SC

MENU

Baked Turkey* (see page 108)
Cornbread Dressing * (see page 71)
Giblet Gravy* (see page 175)
Green Beans
Fried Corn*
Frozen Cranberry Salad* (see page 50)
Souffléed Sweet Potatoes*
Squash Casserole* (see page 64)
Aronowitz Fruitcake*
Grandma Maggie's Coconut Pie* or Impossible Pie*

recipe included

FRIED CORN

1 dozen ears fresh corn
3 tablespoons bacon drippings

Cut kernels from cob. Heat bacon drippings in large skillet. Add corn, and simmer on medium, stirring frequently, until tender. Add water to prevent sticking.
Yield: 8 to 10 servings

SOUFFLÉED SWEET POTATOES

½ cup sugar
1 stick butter, melted
½ cup light corn syrup
2 eggs
4 large sweet potatoes, cooked, peeled, and mashed
Butter

TOPPING

1 cup firmly packed light brown sugar
⅓ cup all-purpose flour
5 tablespoons butter, melted
1 cup chopped pecans

Combine sugar, and next 3 ingredients. Stir in potatoes. Butter a 2-quart casserole. Spoon potatoes into casserole. To make topping, combine all ingredients and mix well. Sprinkle topping over potatoes. Bake at 350° for 30 minutes.
Yield: 4 to 6 servings

ARONOWITZ FRUITCAKE

1 pound pitted dates, chopped
1 pound pecans, chopped
½ pound candied pineapple, chopped
¼ pound candied red cherries, chopped
¼ pound candied green cherries, chopped
1 cup sugar
1 cup all-purpose flour
2 teaspoons baking powder
1 teaspoon nutmeg
½ teaspoon salt
4 eggs
1 teaspoon vanilla
Butter

Combine dates, and next 4 ingredients in large bowl. Set aside.
Combine sugar, and next 4 ingredients. Add dry ingredients to fruit
mixture, stirring well. Beat eggs with vanilla; add to fruit mixture.
Grease 2 loaf pans with butter. Line with brown paper. Spoon batter
into loaf pans. Bake at 250° for 2 hours.
Yield: 18 to 20 servings

GRANDMA MAGGIE'S COCONUT PIE

½ stick butter
1 cup sugar
2 eggs
2 tablespoons cornstarch or all-purpose flour
¾ cup milk
1 cup coconut
2 teaspoons lemon or vanilla extract
1 (9-inch) pie shell, unbaked

Cream butter and sugar. Add eggs, cornstarch, milk, and coconut. Mix
well. Add flavoring. Pour batter into pie shell. Bake at 375° for 30
minutes.
Yield: 8 servings

As a citizen and combat veteran of WW II, what America means to me may be summed up in two words: freedom and opportunity. Freedom to worship God without fear or interference; freedom to come and go without governmental restrictions; freedom to have and express political views without endangerment to yourself or your family; freedom to own firearms. The opportunity to be what you can be; the opportunity of meeting your responsibilities of citizenship as an American. I cannot imagine not being an American.

Gene Denton
Oark, AR

IMPOSSIBLE PIE

3 eggs
½ stick margarine, melted
1 (8-ounce) can crushed pineapple, drained
1 cup unsweetened coconut
½ cup sugar
1 cup self-rising flour
¼ cup milk, if needed
½ cup crushed pecans
Butter, as needed

Mix eggs with next 5 ingredients. Add milk if mixture is not too soupy. Top with pecans. Butter a 10-inch pie plate; pour in mixture. Bake at 350° for 45 minutes, or until lightly browned and crust has formed.
Yield: 8 servings

LOOSEN YOUR BELT

Desserts You Can't Pass Up

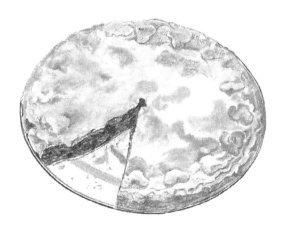

Peter Rivis ©1995

I've been hunting turkeys since I was eight years old. My daddy would load the family in the wagon, and we'd camp across Piney River. He'd take me with him in the early morning. I suspect I'm the oldest woman turkey hunter in Missouri.

I started turkey hunting with a 16 gauge shotgun, but now I shoot a 12 gauge. I only take one shot. I won't shoot over 20 yards. I want that bird to drop in his tracks. Everyone I hunt with knows this. When they hear one shot in the turkey woods, they figure, "Well, Aileen's got her bird."

I hunt every minute of every day. I get there early, but if I get sleepy, I go to sleep. One fall, I woke up and there were turkeys all around me. I mean, I was one of 'em! They were going "prrrrttt? prrrrttt?" Thought they'd really found something.

Aileen Hatch, 82
Plato, MO

PERSIMMON PUDDING

¼ **teaspoon baking soda**
1 **cup all-purpose flour**
1 **teaspoon baking powder**
½ **teaspoon cinnamon or nutmeg**
¼ **teaspoon salt**
½ **cup persimmon pulp**
1 **cup sugar**
1 **egg**
½ **stick margarine, softened**
1½ **cups milk**
Nonstick cooking spray

Sift baking soda, and next 4 ingredients together. Push persimmon pulp through colander. Discard seeds and skin. Mix sugar, egg, margarine, milk, and persimmon pulp. Slowly add dry mixture into persimmon mixture, and blend well. Coat an 8-inch square pan with nonstick cooking spray. Pour persimmon mixture into pan. Bake at 350° for 1 hour.
Yield: 8 servings

APPLE CAKE

Butter, as needed
5 to 6 apples, pared and sliced
⅓ cup sugar
½ teaspoon cinnamon
2 eggs
1 cup sugar
½ cup vegetable oil
1⅓ cups all-purpose flour
½ teaspoon baking powder
1 teaspoon vanilla

Grease a 11x7x1½-inch baking dish. Arrange apples in dish. Combine sugar and cinnamon, and sprinkle over apples. Cream eggs, sugar, and oil. Mix remaining ingredients into egg mixture. Spread over apples. Bake at 350° for 40 to 45 minutes.
Yield: 8 to 10 servings

Audrey Zimmerman
Alburtis, PA

IOWA CHOCOLATE CAKE

¾ cup shortening
2 cups sugar
1½ cups boiling water
2 cups all-purpose flour
2 teaspoons baking soda
½ cup cocoa
½ teaspoon salt
2 eggs, beaten
1 teaspoon vanilla
Butter, as needed

Put shortening and sugar into a mixing bowl. Cover with water. Sift flour, and next 3 ingredients twice. Mix into hot mixture. Blend in eggs and vanilla. Batter will be very thin. Butter a 13x9x2-inch rectangular pan. Pour mixture into pan. Bake at 350°for 35 to 45 minutes, or until cake pulls away from sides of pan.
Yield: 8 to 10 servings

Jean Aikin
Hills, IA

MINNESOTA CHOCOLATE CAKE

2 cups all-purpose flour
1¼ cups sugar
½ cup cocoa
1 teaspoon salt
1 tablespoon baking soda
1 cup buttermilk
1 cup strong black coffee
⅔ cup vegetable oil
1 egg
1 teaspoon vanilla

FROSTING

1 cup sugar
3 tablespoons cornstarch
½ teaspoon salt
1 to 2 squares baking chocolate
1 cup water
1 teaspoon vanilla
3 tablespoons butter

For cake, mix ingredients in order listed. Batter will be runny. Bake in a 13x9x2-inch pan at 350° for 30 to 40 minutes, or until center springs back. To make frosting, heat all ingredients in a saucepan until it thickens. Frost cake while both it and frosting are hot.
Yield: 8 to 10 servings

Cindy Ballard
Des Moines, IA

CHOCOLATE ZUCCHINI CAKE

½ cup soft margarine
½ cup vegetable oil
1¾ cup sugar
2 eggs
1 teaspoon vanilla
½ cup buttermilk
2½ cups unsifted all-purpose flour
4 tablespoons cocoa
½ teaspoon baking powder
½ teaspoon cinnamon
½ teaspoon ground cloves
1 teaspoon baking soda
½ teaspoon salt
2 cups shredded zucchini, seeded
Butter, as needed
Flour, as needed
1 cup chocolate chips

Cream margarine, oil, and sugar. Add eggs, vanilla, and buttermilk. Beat well. Mix together flour, and next 6 ingredients; add to egg mixture. Beat well with mixer. Stir in zucchini. Grease and flour a 13x9x2-inch rectangular pan. Spoon batter into pan. Sprinkle with chocolate chips. Bake at 325° for 40 to 45 minutes, or until toothpick comes out clean and dry.

This cake is moist and tender, and needs no frosting.
Large zucchini work best. If skin is tender, leave unpeeled.
Yield: 18 servings

Jan Welker
Olympia, WA

MOTHER'S OH AND AH CAKE

3 (1-ounce) squares semisweet chocolate
1 cup hot water
1 teaspoon red food coloring
1½ teaspoons baking soda
2 cups sugar
½ cup shortening
3 eggs
½ teaspoon salt
2½ cups all-purpose flour
1 cup sour cream
Butter, as needed
Flour, as needed

CREAMY ICING

5 tablespoons all-purpose flour
1 cup milk
1 cup sugar
1 teaspoon vanilla
1 stick butter, softened
1 stick margarine, softened

Melt chocolate in water. Cool. Add food coloring and soda; set aside.
In large bowl, cream sugar and next 5 ingredients. Add chocolate
mixture. Grease and flour three, 9-inch round cake pans. Pour mixture
into pans. Bake at 350° for 40 to 45 minutes, or until toothpick
inserted in center comes out clean. To make icing, in a medium
saucepan, stir flour into milk, and heat until thickened. Cool. In
mixing bowl, cream sugar with remaining ingredients; add milk
mixture. Beat until creamy. Frost cake between layers and around sides
and top.
Yield: 14 to 16 servings

Helen "Mom" Rosenlieb
Clay City, IL

BLUEBERRY CAKE

½ stick butter
1 cup sugar
1 egg, well beaten
1½ cups all-purpose flour
2 teaspoons baking powder
½ cup milk
½ teaspoon almond extract
1 cup fresh or frozen blueberries (thawed and drained)
Butter, as needed

TOPPING

½ teaspoon cinnamon
2 tablespoons sugar
2 tablespoons melted butter

Cream butter and sugar. Blend in egg. Mix flour with baking powder; add to creamed mixture, alternating with milk mixed with flavoring. Beat until smooth. Fold in blueberries. Grease an 8-inch square pan. Pour mixture into pan. For topping, combine cinnamon and next 2 ingredients. Sprinkle over top. Bake at 350° for 25 to 30 minutes, or until toothpick inserted into center comes out clean.
Yield: 4 to 6 servings

VerDonna Otey
Makanda, IL

GOOEY BUTTER CAKE

1 (18.25-ounce) package yellow cake mix
2 eggs
1 stick butter, softened

FROSTING

1 teaspoon vanilla
1 (16-ounce) box powdered sugar
2 eggs
1 (8-ounce) package cream cheese, softened

Mix cake mix with eggs and butter. Spread into a 13x9x2-inch pan. For frosting, mix remaining ingredients; spread atop cake mixture. Bake at 350° for 35 to 40 minutes.
Yield: 15 servings

VerDonna Otey
Makanda, IL

GRANDPA'S FAVORITE CAKE

4 eggs
2 cups sugar
2 cups cake flour
2 teaspoons baking powder
1 cup milk
2 tablespoons butter
2 teaspoons vanilla

ICING

7 tablespoons brown sugar
5 tablespoons butter
3 tablespoons heavy cream
Coconut

Beat eggs until very light. Add sugar, and continue beating. Sift together flour and baking powder; add to egg mixture. Boil milk and butter; add to batter while hot. Stir in vanilla. Bake in a 13x9x2-inch pan at 300° for 25 to 30 minutes. To make icing, heat brown sugar and butter until melted; blend in cream. Spread on cake while cake is still hot. Sprinkle with coconut, and brown under broiler.
Watch carefully to prevent coconut from burning.
Yield: 15 servings

Peggy Leib
Honeoye Falls, NY

CHOCOLATE POUND CAKE

2 sticks butter
½ cup shortening
3 cups sugar
5 eggs
4 heaping tablespoons cocoa
3 cups all-purpose flour
1 teaspoon baking powder
Pinch of salt
1 cup milk
1 tablespoon vanilla

With electric mixer, cream butter, and next 3 ingredients. Sift cocoa, and next 3 ingredients into a large bowl. Combine milk and vanilla. Alternately incorporate wet mixtures into dry mixture until well blended. Grease a Bundt pan, and bake at 325° for 1 hour and 15 minutes, or until toothpick comes out clean.
Yield: 10 to 12 servings

Jim Parker
Longview, TX

TURTLE CAKE

1 box German chocolate cake mix
¾ cup butter
1 cup evaporated milk
1 (14-ounce) package caramels
1 cup chopped pecans, divided
1 cup semi-sweet chocolate chips

Prepare cake mix as directed. Pour ¼ to ½ of batter into 13x9x2-inch baking pan coated with cooking spray. Bake at 350° for 15 minutes. Melt butter, milk, and caramels in a saucepan and pour over partially cooked batter. Sprinkle half of pecans and all of chocolate chips over caramel mixture. Pour on remaining batter. Sprinkle with remaining nuts. Bake 20 to 25 minutes longer.
Yield: 10 to 12 servings

Dottie McGirt
Lexington, NC

SUNSHINE CAKE

1 box yellow cake mix
⅓ cup vegetable oil
4 eggs
1 can mandarin oranges, undrained
1 (5⅝-ounce) package instant vanilla pudding
1 (16-ounce) can crushed pineapple, undrained
1 (8-ounce) container frozen whipped topping

Mix first 4 ingredients, beating 2 minutes. Bake in three 8-inch cake pans at 350° for 20 to 25 minutes. Cool layers completely. Beat pudding and ¾ of the pineapple and its juice (save remaining pineapple for other uses). Fold in whipped topping. Spread between cake layers and on top. Keep refrigerated.
Yield: 12 servings

Leslie Sapp
FL

PISTACHIO CAKE

1 box yellow cake mix
1 (5⅝-ounce) box pistachio instant pudding mix
¾ cup water
½ cup corn oil
4 eggs
1 teaspoon butter flavoring
1 teaspoon almond flavoring

Mix together cake mix and pudding mix. Stir in water, corn oil, eggs, and flavorings. Beat at medium speed for 2 to 3 minutes until smooth and well blended. Bake in a greased Bundt pan at 350° for 55 to 60 minutes.
Yield: 12 servings

Shannon Tollison
Edgefield, SC

CHOCOLATE
SOUR CREAM BROWNIES

2 cups all-purpose flour
2 cups sugar
4 tablespoons cocoa
1 teaspoon baking soda
1 scant teaspoon cinnamon
1 stick margarine
½ cup shortening
1 cup water
1 teaspoon vinegar
½ cup milk
2 eggs
1 teaspoon vanilla
Nonstick cooking spray
Flour, as needed

FROSTING

1 stick margarine
6 tablespoons milk
4 tablespoons cocoa
1 (16-ounce) box powdered sugar

Sift flour and next 4 ingredients. Boil margarine and shortening in water; pour over dry ingredients. Stir vinegar into milk. Add milk, eggs, and vanilla to other mixture. Coat a 13x9x2-inch pan with nonstick cooking spray. Dust with flour. Pour batter into pan. Bake at 350° for 22 minutes. To make frosting, bring margarine, milk, and cocoa to a boil; then stir in powdered sugar. Spread over brownies. **Yield**: 15 to 18 servings

Ivy Coffey
Russell, IA

DANCIN' GRANNY'S PUMPKIN CAKE ROLL

3 eggs
1 cup sugar
⅔ cup pumpkin
1 teaspoon lemon juice
¾ cup all-purpose flour
1 teaspoon baking powder
2 teaspoons cinnamon
1 teaspoon ground ginger
½ teaspoon ground nutmeg
½ teaspoon salt
Butter, as needed
Flour, as needed
1 cup finely chopped walnuts or pecans
Powdered sugar, as needed

FILLING

1 cup powdered sugar
2 (3-ounce) packages cream cheese, softened
4 tablespoons butter
½ teaspoon vanilla

Beat eggs on high speed of mixer for 5 minutes. Gradually beat in sugar. Stir in pumpkin and lemon juice. In a small bowl, stir together flour, and next 5 ingredients; fold into pumpkin mixture. Grease and flour a 13x9x2-inch rectangular pan. Spread into pan. Top with chopped nuts. Bake at 375° for 15 minutes. Sprinkle a towel with powdered sugar. Turn out cake onto towel. Starting at narrow end, roll towel and cake together. When cool, unroll. Make filling by beating powdered sugar, and next 3 ingredients until smooth. Spread over cake; roll. Chill.
To serve, cut into slices.
Yield: 15 to 18 servings

Helen "Mom" Rosenlieb
Clay City, IL

PUMPKIN PIE SQUARES

CRUST

1 cup all-purpose flour
½ cup quick oats
½ cup brown sugar
1 stick margarine
Nonstick cooking spray

FILLING

1 (16-ounce) can pumpkin
2 eggs
1 (5-ounce) can evaporated milk
¾ cup sugar
½ teaspoon salt
1 teaspoon cinnamon
½ teaspoon ground ginger

Mix flour, and next 3 ingredients until crumbly. Coat a 13x9x2-inch pan with nonstick cooking spray. Press crust onto bottom of pan. Bake at 350˚ for 15 minutes. To make filling, mix all ingredients and pour over crust. Bake at 350° for an additional 35 minutes.
Yield: 12 to 15 servings

Susie Brown
Edgefield, SC

APPLE CRUMB PIE

4 large tart apples, cored, pared, and sliced
⅔ cup sugar
2 tablespoons butter
Juice from ½ lemon

TOPPING

1 stick butter, softened
¼ cup brown sugar
¼ cup sugar
1 cup all-purpose flour

Place apple slices in pie plate. Top with sugar and butter. Pour lemon juice on top. Lightly toss ingredients. Using fingers, mix ingredients for topping; then crumble over apples. Bake at 400° for 20 minutes. Lower heat, and bake 15 minutes more.
Serve hot. Top with whipped cream or ice cream, if desired.
Yield: 6 servings

James Earl and Mary Kennamer
Edgefield, SC

205

STRAWBERRY CHOCOLATE PIE

3 (1-ounce) squares semisweet chocolate, divided
1 tablespoon butter
1 (9-inch) pie shell, baked
2 (3-ounce) packages cream cheese, softened
½ cup sour cream
3 tablespoons sugar
½ teaspoon vanilla
3 to 4 cups strawberries, hulled
⅓ cup strawberry jam, melted

In a small saucepan, melt 2 squares chocolate and butter over low heat, stirring constantly. Brush over bottom and sides of the pie shell. Chill. In a mixing bowl, beat cream cheese and next 3 ingredients until smooth. Spread over chocolate layer. Chill 2 hours. Arrange strawberries, tip end up, over filling. Brush jam over strawberries. Melt remaining chocolate, and drizzle atop pie.
Yield: 6 to 8 servings

Jean Aikin
Hills, IA

FRANKLIN COUNTY SWEET POTATO PIE

2 cups cooked, mashed sweet potatoes
1 (14.5-ounce) can evaporated milk
2 eggs
½ cup brown sugar
½ cup sugar
1 teaspoon cinnamon
¼ teaspoon ground ginger
¼ teaspoon nutmeg
¼ teaspoon allspice
¼ teaspoon ground cloves
¼ teaspoon salt
1 (9-inch) pie shell, unbaked

Combine sweet potatoes and next 10 ingredients. Pour into pie shell. Bake at 425° for 15 minutes; reduce temperature to 350°, and bake 30 to 40 minutes, or until filling is firm.
Yield: 8 servings

Mike Spence
Benton, IL

SHOOFLY PIE

1 cup all-purpose flour
⅔ cup brown sugar
1 tablespoon shortening
1 cup warm water, divided
1 teaspoon baking soda
1 egg, beaten
1 cup molasses
1 (9-inch) pie shell, unbaked

Mix flour and next 2 ingredients until crumbly. In medium bowl, mix ½ cup water with baking soda. Add remaining water, egg, and molasses. Into pie shell, place half the crumb mixture. Top with molasses filling. Top with remaining crumbs. Bake at 350° for 40 to 45 minutes.
Yield: 8 servings

Carrilee Zimmerman
Harrisburg, PA

JAPANESE FRUIT PIE

1 stick butter, softened
1 cup sugar
2 eggs, beaten
Dash of salt
1 tablespoon vinegar
½ cup coconut
½ cup chopped pecans
½ cup raisins
1 (9-inch) pie shell, unbaked

Cream butter and sugar. Add eggs, and next 5 ingredients. Pour into pie shell. Bake at 325° for 35 to 40 minutes.
Yield: 6 to 8 servings

Rose Dameron
Lexington, NC

COCONUT BANANA CREAM PIE

3 cups flaked coconut
7 tablespoons butter or margarine
¾ cup sugar
¼ cup all-purpose flour
3 tablespoons cornstarch
¼ teaspoon salt
3 cups light cream
4 eggs, separated
2½ teaspoons vanilla, divided
2 large, firm bananas
¼ teaspoon cream of tartar
6 tablespoons sugar

In a skillet, saute coconut in butter until golden. Press all but 2 tablespoons into the bottom and up the sides of a greased 9-inch pie pan. Bake at 350° for 7 minutes. In a saucepan, combine ¾ cup sugar, flour, cornstarch, and salt. Gradually add cream, and bring to a boil. Cook and stir constantly for 2 minutes. Add egg yolks, a small amount at a time. Remove from heat; add 2 teaspoons vanilla. Cool to room temperature. Slice bananas on crust; cover with cream mixture. Make meringue by beating egg whites until foamy. Add ½ teaspoon vanilla and cream of tartar. Gradually add 6 tablespoons sugar, beating until stiff peaks form. Immediately spread meringue over pie, sealing to the edge of the pastry. Bake at 350° until meringue is golden brown. Cool completely. If desired, sprinkle remaining 2 tablespoons coconut over meringue.
Yield : 6 to 8 servings

Jean Aikin
Hills, IA

208

CHOCOLATE PIE

2 cups graham cracker crumbs
1 stick butter or margarine
5 tablespoons sugar
2 packages instant chocolate pudding
1 quart vanilla ice cream
1⅓ cups milk
8 ounces whipped topping
2 chocolate candy bars, shaved

Mix first 3 ingredients and press into a 9-inch pie pan. Bake 8 minutes in a 350° oven. Blend next 3 ingredients with mixer. Pour into cooled crust. Chill several hours. Decorate with whipped topping and shaved chocolate. Keep cool.
Yield : 6 to 8 servings

Ivy Coffey
Russell, IA

SPICY PUMPKIN PIE

1 egg white
1 pint pumpkin
¾ cup sugar
½ teaspoon cinnamon
Dash nutmeg
1 cup milk
½ teaspoon salt
1 9-inch pie crust, unbaked

Beat egg white. Add next 6 ingredients. Pour into pie crust. Bake for 1 hour at 400°.
Yield : 6 to 8 servings

Ivy Coffey
Russell, IA

FRIED PIES

FILLING

1 (16-ounce) package dried fruit (peaches, apricots, or apples)
1½ cups sugar

CRUST

4 cups all-purpose flour
1 teaspoon salt
1 teaspoon baking powder
¼ cup sugar
¾ cup shortening
¾ to 1 cup milk
Flour, as needed

Make filling by placing your choice of dried fruit into a medium saucepan and covering it with water. Simmer until water is evaporated, and fruit is tender. Mash fruit with potato masher, and add sugar while fruit is still hot. Stir well, and refrigerate until cold. Sift flour and next 3 ingredients into a large bowl. Cut in shortening using pastry blender until mixture resembles cornmeal. Stir in milk gradually until dough clings together. Divide dough into fourths. Roll out dough quarters individually on a lightly floured surface to ⅛-inch thick and 10 inches wide. Using a tumbler or large saucer, cut dough into 4- to 5-inch circles. Spoon 1½ tablespoons filling in the center of each circle. Moisten edges with milk; then fold dough over filling to form a semicircle. Seal edges together by pressing with a fork dipped in flour. Heat shortening in a deep fryer to 300°. Submerge one pie at a time in a fryer basket, and fry until brown.
Yield: 12 pies

Clara Denton
Oark, AR

210

PEACH COBBLER

PASTRY

1½ teaspoons salt
3 cups all-purpose flour
1 cup butter-flavored shortening
10 tablespoons ice water

FILLING

2 quarts peaches, peeled and thinly sliced
2 cups sugar
¾ teaspoon nutmeg
2 tablespoons lemon juice
¾ cup all-purpose flour
¼ teaspoon salt
Butter, as needed
Milk, as needed

To make pastry, mix salt with flour. Cut in shortening with a pastry blender until mixture resembles coarse meal. Sprinkle water over surface, 1 tablespoon at a time, and mix in lightly and quickly with a fork, just enough water so pastry holds together. Shape gently into a ball on a lightly floured surface. Divide dough in half. Roll out two, ⅛-inch-thick crusts. Flatten one crust inside a 3-quart baking dish. For filling, combine peaches, 1½ cups sugar (or more, to taste) and next 4 ingredients. Pour over bottom crust. Top with butter. Lay top crust over filling. Brush with a little milk. Bake at 375° for 1 hour.
Yield: 10 to 12 servings

Jim Arthur
Hixson, TN

211

WILD HUCKLEBERRY COBBLER

1 pound fresh huckleberries
1¾ cups sugar
¾ cup water
1 cup self-rising flour
½ cup butter, melted
½ cup milk

Wash and drain berries. Combine berries with sugar and water in a 3-quart saucepan. Crush berries with potato masher to help release juices. Cook over medium heat for about 5 minutes. In a mixing bowl, combine remaining 4 ingredients; mix with a spoon until all lumps are removed. Pour hot berries into a 2½-quart baking dish that has been sprayed with cooking spray. Pour flour mixture evenly over berries. Dot with butter and bake until light golden brown.
Yield : 6 servings
Huckleberries are almost always found during late spring turkey hunting season, so pick them on your way out of the woods. Sometimes they are sweeter than others, so you may have to adjust the sugar accordingly. This cobbler is great topped with ice cream or whipped cream. Blackberries may be substituted.

Kris Gardner
Harpersville, AL

RHUBARB COBBLER

1 teaspoon vinegar
⅔ cup milk
2 cups flour
⅔ cup shortening
⅔ teaspoon soda
½ teaspoon salt
4 to 5 cups diced rhubarb
1¼ cups sugar
½ cup water

Add vinegar to milk to sour it. Combine milk with flour, shortening, soda, and salt to make a dough. Roll out dough to ⅛-inch thickness. Place half the dough in bottom of a greased 2½-quart casserole. Mix rhubarb, sugar, and water. Add to casserole; top mixture with rest of dough, and sprinkle with sugar. Bake at 325° for 1 hour.
Yield : 8 servings

Ivy Coffey
Russell, IA

CHERRY COBBLER

2 sticks plus 2 tablespoons butter or margarine
3½ cups flour, divided
1 cup sugar
1 teaspoon baking powder
1 egg, beaten
2 cans cherry pie filling
½ cup powdered sugar

Mix 1 stick butter, 2 cups flour, 1 cup sugar, baking powder, and egg. Press into bottom of 13x9x2-inch pan. Cover with pie filling. Using your hands, mix remaining butter, flour, and powdered sugar together until crumbly. Sprinkle over cherry filling. Bake at 350° for 45 minutes.
Yield : 12 servings

Paula Von Stein
Hershey, PA

GRANDMA SHUBERT'S BLACKBERRY COBBLER

FILLING

Butter, as needed, divided
5 cups blackberries
1¼ cups sugar
4 tablespoons all-purpose flour

PASTRY

2 cups all-purpose flour
4 tablespoons sugar, divided
4 teaspoons baking powder
½ teaspoon salt
½ teaspoon cream of tartar
½ cup margarine
½ cup milk

Butter a 13x9x2-inch baking dish. Combine blackberries with sugar, and pour into baking dish. Sprinkle flour over berries, and dot with butter. To make pastry, sift flour, 2 tablespoons sugar, and next 3 ingredients into a bowl. Cut in margarine with a pastry blender until mixture resembles coarse meal. Stir in milk with a fork, and form dough into a ball. Roll dough ¼ inch thick. Lay dough over blackberries. Cut a vent in center of dough, and sprinkle top with remaining sugar. Bake at 350° for 40 minutes, or until crust is golden.
Yield: 6 to 8 servings

Marge Shubert
Watson, IL

DATE NUT TORTE

4 eggs
1½ cups sugar
1 cup cake flour
Pinch of salt
1 teaspoon vanilla
1 (16-ounce) box pitted dates, chopped
4 cups chopped pecans

Cream eggs and sugar in mixing bowl. Add flour, and remaining ingredients. Blend well. Pour into two 9-inch torte pans. Bake at 350° for 40 minutes. Cool.
Yield: 20 servings

Burnell Boyd
Tifton, GA

CHEESE DANISH

Nonstick cooking spray
2 (8-count) packages refrigerated crescent rolls, divided
2 (8-ounce) packages cream cheese, softened
¾ cup sugar
1 teaspoon vanilla
1 egg, beaten

Coat a 13x9x2-inch square pan with nonstick cooking spray. Place rolls from 1 package in the pan. Mix cream cheese with remaining ingredients until creamy, and spoon over rolls in pan. Place other package of rolls over mixture. Bake at 300° for 25 minutes, or until brown.
Yield: 10 to 12 servings

Sandy Miller
Edgefield, SC

GLYNN'S OATMEAL COOKIES

4 sticks margarine
4 eggs
2⅓ cups brown sugar
1⅔ cups sugar
2 teaspoons vanilla
3 cups all-purpose flour, sifted
6 cups old-fashioned oatmeal
2 teaspoons baking powder
1 teaspoon salt
1½ cups raisins
1½ cups chopped pecans

Cream margarine. Beat in eggs, and next 3 ingredients. In a large bowl, add creamed mixture and remaining ingredients; mix thoroughly. Drop by teaspoonfuls, 1 inch apart, on ungreased cookie sheets, and bake at 350° until golden, about 15 minutes.
Yield: 15 dozen cookies

Glynn Shubert
Watson, IL

215

SAND TARTS

½ cup butter
1 cup sugar
1 egg, beaten
2 cups cake flour
2 teaspoons baking powder
1 teaspoon salt
1 egg white, beaten
1 teaspoon cinnamon
1 teaspoon sugar
1 tablespoon chopped nuts

Cream butter and sugar thoroughly. Add egg and next 3 ingredients. Chill dough until stiff. Roll out and cut with cookie cutters. Brush tops with egg whites. Sprinkle with cinnamon, sugar, and nuts. Bake on ungreased cookie sheets at 375° for 10 minutes.
Yield: about 2 to 3 dozen

Phyllis V. Keck
Mountville, PA

JAN'S CRISPY RICE COOKIES

1 cup sugar
1 cup brown sugar
1 cup shortening
2 eggs
1 cup coconut
2 cups all-purpose flour
1 teaspoon baking powder
1 teaspoon baking soda
1 teaspoon salt
1 teaspoon vanilla
2 cups crispy rice cereal
1 cup chopped pecans or walnuts

Cream sugars and shortening until fluffy. Stir in eggs and coconut. Mix in flour, and next 4 ingredients. Fold in cereal and nuts. Drop dough by teaspoonfuls onto cookie sheet, and bake at 350° for 8 to 10 minutes, or until golden.
Yield: about 3 dozen

Janice Crackel
Olney, IL

MONSTER COOKIES

3 eggs
½ cup brown sugar
1 cup sugar
1 stick margarine
1 tablespoon vanilla
1¼ cups peanut butter
4½ cups oatmeal
2 teaspoon baking soda
½ cup chocolate-coated chocolate pieces
½ cup chocolate chips
½ cup chopped pecans or walnuts

Mix all ingredients. Bake at 350° for 8 to 10 minutes. Watch closely because they burn easily on bottom.
Yield: 3 dozen

Ivy Coffey
Russell, IA

BANANA NUGGET COOKIES

1½ cups all-purpose flour
1 cup sugar
½ teaspoon baking soda
1 teaspoon salt
¼ teaspoon nutmeg
¾ teaspoon cinnamon
¾ cup shortening
1 egg, beaten
1 cup mashed bananas
1¾ cup oatmeal
1 cup chocolate chips

Sift together flour, and next 5 ingredients. Cut in shortening and egg. Add banana, and remaining ingredients. Beat until well mixed. Drop by teaspoonfuls onto ungreased cookie sheet. Bake at 375° for 15 minutes, or until golden. Do not overbake.
Yield: 3 dozen cookies

Doris McKinney
Roann, IN

217

CHOCOLATE CHIP COOKIES

2 cups sugar
2 cups packed brown sugar
2 cups shortening, melted
6 eggs
4 teaspoons baking soda
2 teaspoons vanilla
Salt, as desired
1 (12-ounce) package semisweet chocolate chips
1 (12-ounce) package milk chocolate chips
7 cups all-purpose flour
Butter, as needed

Mix sugar, and next 9 ingredients in order given. Grease 2 cookie sheets with butter. Drop by tablespoonfuls onto cookie sheets. Bake at 325° for 9 to 11 minutes.
Yield: 5 to 6 dozen

Leah Glines
Coon Rapids, MN

TURKEY TORTE

½ cup Wild Turkey Liqueur
28 graham cracker squares, each broken into 2 pieces
¾ cup apricot preserves
1 (12-ounce) package semisweet chocolate chips
1 (14-ounce) can sweetened condensed milk
4 ounces heavy cream
1 tablespoon instant coffee
Slivered almonds

Pour liqueur into a 9-inch pie plate. Dip half the graham crackers into liqueur. Place on cookie sheet covered by wax paper. Spread on apricot preserves; top with other half of graham crackers. In medium saucepan, heat chocolate, milk, and heavy cream. Stir in coffee. Cool. Spread top and sides of crackers. Garnish with almonds. Chill at least 8 hours, or overnight.
Yield: 14 servings

Austin Nichols Distilling Co.
Lawrenceburg, KY

KATIE BRAHM'S FRUIT PUDDING CRÊPES

CRÊPES

½ cup all-purpose flour
¼ teaspoon salt
2 eggs, lightly beaten
½ cup milk
1 tablespoon cold water
1 tablespoon melted butter
Vegetable oil, as needed

FILLING

1 (3-ounce) package instant vanilla pudding
1 cup milk
1 (8-ounce) carton frozen whipped topping
4 cups fresh fruit (strawberries, blueberries, peaches, etc.), peeled
  and thinly sliced

Sift flour and salt together into a bowl. Mix eggs and next 3
ingredients, and add slowly to dry ingredients, beating until smooth.
Let stand at room temperature for 15 minutes. Brush bottom and
sides of a heavy 6-inch skillet with oil, and set over moderate heat for
30 seconds. Stir batter; then add 2 tablespoons to the skillet, tipping it
back and forth so batter just coats bottom. Brown lightly on one side,
about 30 seconds, and brown other side. Remove, and cool on paper
towels. Repeat with remaining batter. For filling, mix pudding, milk,
and whipped topping. Fold in fruit. To serve, place a generous
spoonful of filling on each crêpe, and roll up to enclose filling.
Top with additional whipped topping and a piece of fruit, if desired.
Yield: 10 servings

Shirley Grenoble
Altoona, PA

219

FRUIT DELIGHT

1 cantaloupe
2 peaches
1 honeydew melon
2 bananas
1 small watermelon

SAUCE

1 peach, peeled and seeded
1 ripe banana, peeled
3 tablespoons honey
1 tablespoon lemon juice

Remove rind or peel, and seed as necessary. Cube fruit. To make
sauce, purée peach and remaining ingredients in blender. Place fruit in
individual dishes. Pour small amount of sauce over fruit, and serve
immediately.
Yield: 10 to 12 servings (1 cup sauce and about 5 to 6 cups fruit)

Dennis Campbell
Waynesboro, VA

JAN'S ESCALLOPED PINEAPPLE

1 cup milk
4 cups soft breadcrumbs
3 eggs
1 cup sugar
1 stick margarine, melted
1 (29-ounce) can crushed pineapple, drained

Pour milk over breadcrumbs. Cream eggs and sugar; blend in
margarine. Combine both mixtures. Stir in pineapple. Pour into a 1½-
quart baking dish. Bake at 325° for 45 minutes.
Yield: 4 to 6 servings

Janice Crackel
Olney, IL

LAYERED CHOCOLATE DELIGHT

1 cup all-purpose flour
½ cup chopped nuts
1 stick margarine
1 (8-ounce) package cream cheese, softened
1 cup powdered sugar
1 (16-ounce) container frozen whipped topping, divided
2 (3-ounce) packages instant chocolate pudding
3 cups milk

Blend flour, nuts, and margarine until smooth. Spread onto 13x9x2-inch pan. Bake at 350° for 10 minutes. Cool. Mix cream cheese with sugar and half the whipped topping. Spread atop crust. Mix pudding and milk. Spread atop cream cheese layer. Top with remaining whipped topping. Refrigerate at least 8 hours, or overnight.
Yield: 12 servings

Velma Brown
Clearfield, PA

TURKEY SWIRL

½ pint vanilla ice cream
½ pint chocolate ice cream
¼ cup Wild Turkey Liqueur
Chopped nuts
Miniature marshmallows
Chopped maraschino cherries

Blend ice creams and liqueur until smooth. Pour into dessert glasses. Garnish with nuts, marshmallows, and cherries.
Yield: 4 to 6 servings

Austin Nichols Distilling Co.
Lawrenceburg, KY

When I came on board as a member, and later was elected to the board of directors, my goal was to help build the National Wild Turkey Federation into an organization so strong that the wild turkey will never be in jeopardy. As a hunter, I understand the need to hunt safely and in a spirit of fair chase. As a veterinarian, I understand the research aspect of wildlife management. Although I've hunted big game on four continents, turkey hunting is my favorite form of hunting. That's why I want to help perpetuate it for future generations of Americans.

George W. Dykes
Safford, AL

LAYERED PEACH DELIGHT

2 cups self-rising flour
2 sticks margarine, melted
1 cup chopped pecans or walnuts
1 (8-ounce) package cream cheese, softened
2½ cups powdered sugar
1 (8-ounce) carton frozen whipped topping, slightly thawed
4 cups fresh peaches, sliced
1 cup sugar
4 tablespoons all-purpose flour
4 tablespoons peach jello
1 cup water

Combine flour, margarine, and nuts. Spread onto a 13x9x2-inch rectangular pan. Bake at 375° for 15 to 20 minutes, or until lightly browned. Cool completely. Mix cream cheese, powdered sugar, and whipped topping, and spread onto crust. Place peaches evenly over cream cheese layer. Combine sugar, and next 2 ingredients. Stir in water. Cook over medium heat until thick and clear; cool completely. Pour over peaches, and refrigerate at least 8 hours, or overnight.
Yield: 12 servings

HUNTING THE
BASICS ON
TURKEY

INDEX

5 SUBSPECIES OF WILD TURKEYS IN THE UNITED STATES

PHOTO CREDIT: BILL KINNEY

EASTERN WILD TURKEY
(Meleagris gallopavo silvestris)

The Eastern wild turkey is the most widely distributed, abundant, and hunted turkey subspecies found in the United States. It inhabits roughly the eastern half of the country. The Eastern wild turkey is found in hardwood and mixed forests from New England and southern Canada to northern Florida and west to Texas, Missouri, Iowa, and Minnesota. It has also been successfully transplanted in California, Oregon, and Washington, states outside its suspected original range.

Because it ranges the farthest north, Eastern wild turkeys can also grow to be among the largest. Adult males may measure up to 4 feet tall and weigh more than 20 pounds. Tail feathers are tipped with dark buff or chocolate brown. In contrast, breast feathers are tipped in black. Other body feathers are characterized by rich, metallic, copper/bronze iridescence.

PHOTO CREDIT: LOVETT E. WILLIAMS, JR.

FLORIDA WILD TURKEY
(Meleagris gallopavo osceola)

The Florida wild turkey, also referred to as the Osceola, is found only on the peninsula of Florida. It's similar to the eastern wild turkey but is smaller and darker in color with less white veining in the wing quills. The white bars in these feathers are narrow, irregular, and broken and do not extend all the way to the feather shaft.

Feathers of the Florida turkey show more iridescent green and red colors, with less bronze than the eastern. The dark color of the tail coverts and the large tail feathers tipped in brown are similar to the eastern, but unlike the lighter colors of the three western subspecies. Its colorations and behavior are ideal for the flat pine woods, oak and palmetto hammocks, and swamp habitats of Florida.

RIO GRANDE WILD TURKEY
(Meleagris gallopavo intermedia)

The Rio Grande wild turkey is native to the central plains states and got its common name from the area in which it is found—the life-giving water supply that borders the brushy scrub, arid country of the southern Great Plains, western Texas, and northeastern Mexico. The Rio inhabits brush areas near streams and rivers or mesquite, pine, and scrub oak forests. It may be found up to 6,000 feet elevations and generally favors more open country.

It is similar in general appearance to the other subspecies of the wild turkey and similar in body size to the Eastern subspecies, about 4 feet tall, but with disproportionately long legs. Rio Grande turkeys are comparatively pale and copper colored. They are distinguished from the eastern and Florida subspecies by having tail feathers and tail/rump coverts tipped with yellowish-buff or tan color rather than medium or dark brown.

MERRIAM'S WILD TURKEY
(Meleagris gallopavo merriami)

The Merriam's wild turkey is found primarily in the ponderosa pine, western mountain regions of the United States. Within its suspected historic range in Arizona, New Mexico, and Colorado, the Merriam's was relatively isolated from the other subspecies of wild turkey. It has been successfully stocked beyond its natural range in the Rocky Mountains and outside of the mountains into Nebraska, Washington, California, Oregon, and other areas.

Adult males are clearly distinguished from the Eastern, Florida, and Rio Grande by the nearly white feathers on the lower back and tail feather margins. Its size is comparable to the Eastern turkey, but has a blacker appearance with blue, purple, and bronze reflections. The Merriam's appears to have a white rump due to its pinkish, buff, or whitish tail coverts and tips.

GOULD'S WILD TURKEY
(Meleagris gallopavo mexicana)

The fifth recognized, but least known, wild turkey subspecies is the Gould's, found in portions of Arizona and New Mexico as well as northern Mexico. Like the Merriam's, the Gould's is a bird of the mountains. It exists in very small numbers in Arizona and New Mexico along the U.S./Mexico border, but is apparently abundant in the northwestern portions of Mexico.

The Gould's turkey is the largest of the 5 subspecies and somewhat resembles the Merriam's turkey. It has longer legs, larger feet, and larger center tail feathers than any of the other wild turkey subspecies in North America. Gould's differ by having distinctive white tips on the tail feathers and tail rump coverts, which usually separate to show an "eyelash" appearance. Lower back and rump feathers have copper and greenish-golden reflection, while the body plumage is said to be somewhat blue-green in coloration.

SKINNIN' OLE TOM

For several springs and falls, I held the traditional opinion that no turkey was fit for the table without its skin fully intact. After the hunt. I laboriously plucked each trophy, though it was a lengthy chore not enjoyed after a short night, rocky ridges, and stretched nerves.

It was the late Wayne Kochenderfer, host of one of the finest turkey hunting camps in northern Pennsylvania, who offered to show me a "fast and simple" cleaning method after a bearded but tiring day on Young Woman's Creek during the fall of 1969. I was all eyes. The method was easy, and I've used it ever since.

The choice of skinning or plucking depends largely on the method of cooking you plan to use. Some types of cooking tend to dry out the flesh of the bird; therefore, the moisture-sealing skin should be left on. Yet other treatments of the skinless bird render it moist and tender. My choices of preparation, either deep frying or grilling, don't require the skin to be intact.

With a little practice, the entire operation shown here takes less than 10 minutes. This method of preparation also removes much of the cholesterol and fat that tends to concentrate in the skin.

Text: Rob Keck / Photos: Jay Langston

STEP ONE: *After hanging the bird by the head and plucking or cutting the beard from the chest, you're ready to remove the appendages. Beginning with the legs, apply pressure on the front of one, thus straining the joint. Sever the skin and tendons at the knuckle. Repeat the procedure on the other.*

STEP TWO: *Extend the wing parallel to the ground. At the second joint, slice downward through the feathers, skin, and joint. Twist off the outer wing. Repeat the procedure on the other.*

STEP THREE: *Slice the skin around the neck at the base of the wattles, and work the skin downward and away from the carcass. At the wing bases, work the thumb between the skin and flesh. As the gap enlarges,*

insert one hand around the wing stub and the other around the skin. Pull in opposite directions until the wing stub is skinless. Repeat on the other side. On the lower back, use a knife to separate the thin, tight-clinging skin from the meat.

STEP FOUR: *Cut off the "pope's nose," the bulbous lump that supports the tail feathers.*

STEP FIVE: *Pull the skin from the drumsticks, and use your knife to ease the skin over the end of the bone.*

CUTTING UP THE WHOLE TURKEY

STEPS SIX AND SEVEN: *Remove each leg by cutting through to the hip joint, applying pressure to pop the joint, then finishing the cut. Separate the drumstick from the thigh by cutting through the joint.*

STEP EIGHT: *Next, remove the breast meat, one side at a time. Start at the upper rib cage and carefully cut toward the keel, keeping the blade next to the ribs.*

STEP NINE: *Now you have two choice turkey breast fillets, and you're done except for removing the wing stubs. Finally, cut off the neck for the soup pot and dispose of the bony carcass.*

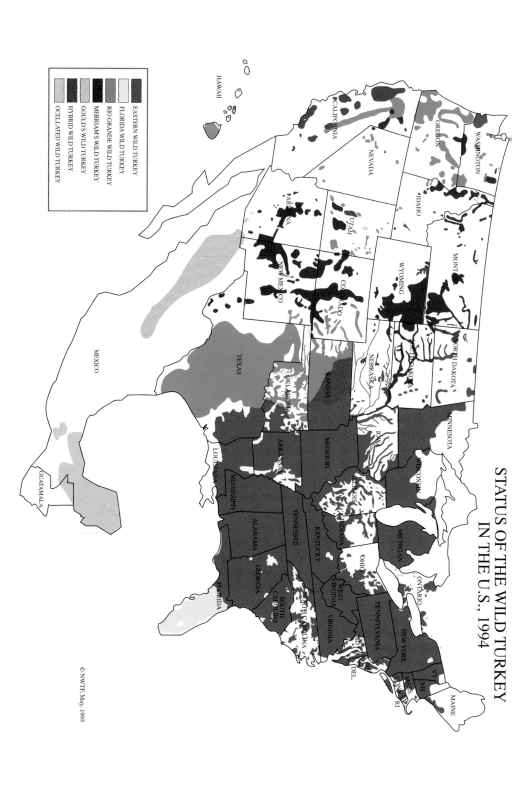

STATUS OF THE WILD TURKEY
IN THE U.S., 1994

EASTERN WILD TURKEY
FLORIDA WILD TURKEY
RIO GRANDE WILD TURKEY
MERRIAM'S WILD TURKEY
GOULD'S WILD TURKEY
HYBRID WILD TURKEY
OCELLATED WILD TURKEY

© NWTF, May, 1995

CLEANING YOUR TURKEY

Which tastes better, wild turkey or domestic? Ask 10 different people and you'll get 10 different answers. One thing for sure, if you don't care for and prepare wild or domestic meat properly, it will not satisfy your taste.

After your bird is dressed, soaking the meat in a tub of cold water will help remove blood from the carcass. Don't add salt to the water. In fact, *Ducks Unlimited* magazine says, "Deviant kitchen behavior is an apt description of the nasty habit of soaking game meats in salt water. So in other words, spare the salt or spoil the meat."

If you are trying to eliminate an unpleasant odor from your bird (indicating improper care in the field), add a teaspoon of baking soda to a generous bowl of cold water and soak for 30 minutes.

Remember to keep your turkey cool, and then clean the bird as soon as possible after the hunt.

Wild turkey is a special treat. To keep it that way, remember to spare the salt.

by Rob Keck

225

SAFELY THAWING A FROZEN TURKEY

Whether you have 4 days or 12 hours, you can safely thaw your frozen turkey without risking bacterial growth. Thawing your turkey in the refrigerator is the preferred method for safety reasons, but you can also thaw it in cold water. The thing to remember about both methods is that they keep your turkey cold while thawing—the key to preventing excessive bacterial growth.

And, no matter which method you select, cook the turkey promptly after thawing.

THAWING IN THE REFRIGERATOR

The following chart shows how long it will take to thaw turkeys of various sizes in the refrigerator. Simply place the turkey in its original wrap on a tray or in a pan to catch moisture that accumulates as it thaws.

THAWING TIME IN THE REFRIGERATOR

Whole Turkey

8 to 12 pounds	1 to 2 days
12 to 16 pounds	2 to 3 days
16 to 20 pounds	3 to 4 days
20 to 24 pounds	4 to 5 days

Pieces of Large Turkey

half, quarter, half breast	1 to 2 days

THAWING IN COLD WATER

If it's the day before you plan to serve your turkey and you just remembered that it's still sitting in the freezer, don't despair. Check the wrapping to make sure there are no tears, and simply place the bird in its unopened bag in the sink or in a large container and cover it with cold water. If the wrapping is torn, place the turkey in another plastic bag, close securely, and then place in water. You will need to change the water frequently to assure safe but effective thawing. The National Turkey Federation recommends every 30 minutes as a rule of thumb.

THAWING TIME IN COLD WATER
Whole turkey

8 to 12 pounds	4 to 6 hours
12 to 16 pounds	6 to 9 hours
16 to 20 pounds	9 to 11 hours
20 to 24 pounds	11 to 12 hours

THAWING IN THE MICROWAVE OVEN

A turkey can also be thawed in a microwave oven. Since microwave ovens vary in what they can accommodate, check the manufacturer's instruction for the size turkey that will fit in your oven, the minutes per pound, and the power level to use for thawing.

MORE POINTERS ON THAWING

Again, remember that frozen, prestuffed turkeys should not be thawed before cooking. Frozen, unstuffed turkeys can also be cooked without being thawed.

If necessary, you can refreeze a partially thawed turkey as long as ice crystals are still visible in the cavity and the neck and giblets remain frozen. However, keep in mind that thawing and refreezing can affect the juiciness and flavor of the turkey.

You may be wondering why thawing your turkey on the kitchen counter isn't recommended. The reason is that room temperatures fall within the danger zone of 60°F to 125°F that promotes active growth of bacteria. Left on a kitchen counter, a frozen turkey will thaw from the outside in. As its surface warms, bacteria multiply. In the time that elapses while the turkey is thawing, the surface bacteria could multiply to dangerous levels. You can't rely on cooking to destroy all bacteria. Some food poisoning organisms produce toxins that withstand heat.

AFTER THE THAWING, WASHING THE TURKEY

Once your turkey has thawed, it requires little preparation before cooking. Remove the neck and giblets from the neck and/or body cavities. Wash the inside and outside of the turkey and the giblets in cold water and drain well. To prevent the spread of bacteria, wash your hands, utensils, and sink after they have come in contact with the raw turkey.

STUFFING A TURKEY

Actually, you can enjoy stuffing with your turkey whether or not you decide to stuff the bird. If you are in a hurry, you may want to bake your stuffing in a greased, covered casserole during the last hour while the turkey roasts.

You'll save time by not stuffing the turkey and having to scoop the stuffing out to serve it once the turkey is done. And an unstuffed turkey takes less time to cook than one that is stuffed.

However, if you prefer to stuff the turkey, read on for some important pointers.

STUFFING POINTERS

It may seem like a good idea to save time by stuffing your turkey in advance, but that's inviting trouble, because harmful bacteria can multiply in the stuffing and cause food poisoning. Turkeys should be stuffed only at the last minute. Dry stuffing ingredients may be prepared the day before, tightly covered, and left at room temperature. The perishables (butter or margarine, mushrooms, oysters, cooked celery and onions, broth) should be refrigerated. The ingredients should then be combined just before stuffing the turkey.

The cavity of the turkey should be stuffed lightly, because stuffing expands as it cooks.

Allow three-fourths of a cup of stuffing for each pound of ready-to-cook turkey. Extra stuffing may be baked separately.

To keep the stuffing in the turkey, you need to close the neck and body cavities. Fold the neck skin over the back and fasten with a skewer, trussing pins, clean string, or toothpicks; twist the wingtips under the back of the turkey to rest against the neck skin. To close the body cavity, use skewers, or tuck ends of legs under a band of skin at the tail, or into metal "hock-locks," if provided, or tie legs together with clean string.

ROASTING A TURKEY

Place the turkey breast side up on a rack in a shallow roasting pan. Do not add water. Before placing the turkey in the oven, you may want to brush it with cooking oil, melted butter or margarine, although this is not necessary. Then cover the turkey with a loose tent of heavy-duty aluminum foil. To make a tent, tear off a sheet of foil 5 to 10 inches longer than the turkey. Crease foil crosswise through the center and place over the turkey; crimping loosely onto sides of pan to hold in place. This prevents overbrowning, allows for maximum heat circulation, keeps the turkey moist, and reduces oven splatter.

When using a meat thermometer, insert it through the foil into the thickest part of the thigh muscle without touching the bone. The inner thigh is the area that heats most slowly. For turkey parts, insert the thermometer in the thickest area.

Roast according to the following chart. To brown the turkey, remove the foil tent 20 to 30 minutes before roasting is finished, and continue cooking until the thermometer registers 185°F.

Basting is usually not necessary during roasting since it cannot penetrate the turkey. Also, opening the oven door frequently prolongs the cooking time.

ROASTING CHART

The following times are based on an oven preheated to 325°F. Plan the roasting time for a large domesticated bird so it will be done about 20 minutes before serving. Use shorter cooking times for wild turkey so it doesn't dry out. Allowing the turkey to stand, covered loosely with aluminum foil, makes the meat easier to carve and juicier.

TIMETABLE FOR ROASTING FRESH OR THAWED DOMESTICATED TURKEY

WEIGHT (pounds)	UNSTUFFED (hours)	STUFFED (hours)
4 to 6 (breasts)	1½ to 2¼	Not applicable
6 to 8	2¼ to 3¼	3 to 3½
8 to 12	3 to 4	3½ to 4½
12 to 16	3½ to 4½	4½ to 5½
16 to 20	4 to 5	5½ to 6½
20 to 24	4½ to 5½	6½ to 7
24 to 28	5 to 6½	7 to 8½
Drumsticks, quarters, thighs	2 to 3½	Not applicable

You should not partially roast a stuffed turkey one day and complete roasting the next. Interrupted cooking enhances the possibility of bacterial growth.

It seems every holiday season brings publicity about a new way of cooking turkey promising excellent results. One that has been publicized recently is long cooking at a very low temperature (250°F). This method is not recommended. Because of the low temperature, the turkey (and stuffing) might take more than 4 hours to reach a high enough temperature to destroy bacteria, and could therefore be unsafe. The quality of the turkey might suffer, too. During prolonged cooking, some areas would tend to become very dry.

TESTING FOR DONENESS

The most reliable method for detecting when your turkey is thoroughly cooked is using a meat thermometer. A whole turkey is done when the temperature reaches 180°F to 185°F in the inner thigh. Dark meat turkey pieces are done at 180°F to 185°F and white meat turkey pieces at 170°F. Stuffing temperature should reach at least 165°F. To check the stuffing, insert the thermometer through the body cavity into the thickest part of the stuffing and leave it for 5 minutes. The stuffing temperature will rise a few degrees after the turkey is removed from the oven.

Another method for testing doneness is to press the fleshy part of the thigh with protected fingers. If the meat feels soft, or if the leg moves up and down easily and the hip joint gives readily or breaks, the turkey is done. Doneness can also be detected by inserting a long-tined fork into thickest area of the inner thigh. If the juices run clear, not pink, turkey is done.

As soon as your turkey is completely cooked, you should remove all stuffing from the cavities. Harmful bacteria is more likely to grow the stuffing if it sits in the bird after cooking. If you do not need the stuffing for first servings, you can put the remaining stuffing in the oven at 200°F to keep hot until you need it.

MICROWAVE COOKING

When microwaving a turkey, check the owner's manual for the size bird that will fit in your oven, and for the time and power level to use. Using an oven cooking bag ensures the most even cooking.

Some microwave ovens do not cook food evenly and "cold spots" develop, especially when cooking dense food like a stuffed turkey. Some sections of the turkey will be done before others are thoroughly cooked, particularly the stuffing. Therefore, microwaving a stuffed turkey is not recommended.

OUTDOOR COOKING

Turkey parts can be cooked on a barbecue grill; a whole turkey or turkey parts can be cooked in a covered kettle grill. Charcoal makes a hot fire. To build your fire, you can line the grill with heavy-duty aluminum foil to aid even cooking and ease cleanup. Stack the coals in a pyramid and follow the directions on the lighter fluid. Once the coals are white-hot, spread the coals to form an even layer.

When using a barbecue grill, be sure racks are 6 to 8 inches from the embers for an even heat without too much intensity. Small turkey quarter roasts are excellent for this method of cooking. Young fryer-roaster turkeys weighing 6 to 8 pounds can be cut into individual servings. The turkey pieces will take at least an hour to cook, depending on the size and thickness. Turn them occasionally while they are cooking. If they start to char, raise the grill farther from the heat.

When using a covered grill, arrange charcoal on both sides of the fire bowl with a drip pan in the center of the coals. Place the whole turkey on a rack over the drip pan. Cover the grill. Add a few coals to each side of the drip pan every hour. To give it a hickory-smoked flavor, sprinkle one-half of a cup of water-soaked hickory chops or flakes over the coals during the last half hour of cooking. If you prefer a heavier hickory-smoked flavor, add more chips or flakes.

You should allow 15 to 18 minutes per pound for an unstuffed turkey cooked on a covered grill. For a stuffed turkey, allow 18 to 24 minutes per pound.

For deep-frying a turkey, see our information on page 115. Commercial deep fryers are available for purchasing.

Smoking a turkey is a slow process with the turkey obtaining flavor from fruit woods. Commercial smokers are available.

ROTISSERIE COOKING

Whole turkeys (unstuffed) can be cooked on a special rotisserie that turns the meat slowly on a rotary spit over direct heat. Since rotisserie vary greatly, follow the directions that come with the equipment.

Before turning on the spit, be sure to balance and mount the bird. See that the turkey does not slip as the spit turns.

To mount a whole turkey on a rotisserie spit, attach the neck skin with a skewer to the back of the body. Tie or skewer the wings close to the body. Insert the spit through the length of the body and tighten the holding prongs. Tie the tail and drumsticks firmly to the rod. If properly balanced, the turkey should rotate evenly when the spit is turned.

TIMETABLE FOR COOKING
TURKEY ON A ROTISSERIE

READY TO COOK WEIGHT	COOKING TIME (hours)
6 to 8 pounds	3 to 3½
8 to 10 pounds	3½ to 4
10 to 12 pounds	4 to 5

THE SECRET OF COOKING
THE TURKEY

(an excerpt from **The Wild Turkey and Its Hunting**
by Edward A. McIlhenny, published in 1914)

Of matters with which the average sportsman has to do, there is none so little understood as that of cooking game, and especially the turkey. Thousands of sportsmen go into the hunting camp expecting to play the role of cook without the knowledge of the simplest requirements and as a consequence are in perpetual trouble and disappointment on account of the blunders that are the inevitable results of lack of information. In the solitude of the forest the hunter should not be at loss for methods of cooking even if he has but a frying pan; a log for a table; his plate, a section of bark or large leaf.

The turkey is supposed to be a bird of dry meat, but this is so only when all juices are boiled or baked out of it. The usual manner in which turkeys are cooked is by roasting or baking. If the turkey is an old one, the first process is to parboil until the flesh is tender; then it is stuffed with sundry things, such as bread-crumbs, oysters, shrimp, shallots, onions, garlic, truffles, red and black pepper, wine and celery to destroy the natural flavor of the bird. It is a mistake to disguise the rich, delicate flavor of turkey meat with the odor of fish, but it is done and called roast turkey.

If the turkey is a young one, cook it in the way usual to stove-baking, after first filling its cavity with a suitable dressing of bread-crumbs, pepper, salt, and onions chopped fine, moistened with fresh country butter. This is the best dressing that can be made, and will detract nothing from the flavor of the bird nor add to it. If an old turkey, parboil it until the flesh is quite tender, then stuff and bake.

In the forest camp, I neither bake nor roast the turkey. Imagine a gobbler dressed and lying on a log or piece of bark beside you. Take a sharp knife, run the blade down alongside the keel bone, removing the flesh from one end of that bone to the other. By this process each half breast can be taken off in two pieces. Lay this slab of white meat skin side down, then begin at the thick end and cut off steaks, transversely, one half inch thick, until all the slab is cut. Now sprinkle with salt and pepper and pile the steaks up together; thus the salt will quickly penetrate. Do not salt any more than you want for one meal; the meat would be ruined if allowed to stand over for the next meal before cooking.

Just as soon as the salt dissolves and the juice begins to flow, spread out the steaks in a pan, sprinkle dry flour lightly on both sides evenly, taking care to do this right, or you will get the flour on too thick. Give the pan a shake and the flour will adjust itself. This flour at once mixes with the juices of the meat, forming a crust around the steak, like batter. Have the frying-pan on the fire with plenty of grease, and sizzling hot so the steak will fry the moment it touches the hot grease. Put the steaks in until the bottom of the pan is covered, but never have one steak lap another. If the grease is quite hot, the steak will soon brown, and when brown on one side, turn, and the moment it is brown on both sides take out of the pan. By this method, you retain almost every particle of the juice of the meat, and at the same time it is brown and crisp, and will nearly melt in the mouth. The flour around the steak does not only prevent the escape of the juice, but also prevents any grease penetrating the meat. If you like gravy, have the frying-pan hot and about a teaspoonful of the grease in which the meat was fried left in it; take a half pint of cold water and pour into the pan. Let this boil about five minutes, when you will have a rich, brown gravy, which season with salt and pepper and pour hot over the steak. You don't want a thing else to eat except some good bread and a cup of Creole coffee. Having eaten turkey thus cooked you would not care for baked or roast turkey again.

CARVING A TURKEY

Remember, you'll get better results carving your turkey if you allow it to stand 20 minutes after you take it out of the oven.

CARVING A TURKEY METHOD 1 (TRADITIONAL METHOD)

1. Remove drumstick and thigh To remove drumstick and thigh, press leg away from body. Joint connecting leg to the hip will oftentimes snap free or may be served easily with knife point. Cut dark meat completely from body by following body contour carefully with knife.

2. Slicing dark meat - Place drumstick and thigh on cutting surface and cut through connecting joint. Both pieces may be individually sliced. Tilt drumstick to convenient angle, slicing towards table as shown in illustration.

3. Slicing thigh - To slice thigh meat, hold firmly on cutting surface with fork. Cut even slices parallel to the bone.

4. Preparing breast In preparing breast for easy slicing, place knife parallel and as close to wing as possible. Make deep cut into breast, cutting right to bone. This is your base cut. All breast slices will stop at this horizontal cut.

235

5. **Carving breasts** - After making base cut, carve downward, ending at base cut. Start each new slice slightly higher up on breast. Keep slices thin and even.

CARVING A TURKEY METHOD 2 (KITCHEN CARVING METHOD)

1. Remove drumstick and thigh by pressing leg away from body. Joint connecting leg to backbone will often snap free or may be severed easily with knife point. Cut dark meat completely from body by following body contour carefully with a knife.

2. Place drumsticks and thigh on separate plate and cut through connecting joint. Both pieces may be individually sliced. Tilt drumsticks to convenient angle, slicing towards plate.

3. To slice thigh meat, hold firmly on plate with fork. Cut even slices parallel to the bone.

4. Remove half of the breast at a time by cutting along keel bone and rib cage with sharp knife.

5. Place half breast on cutting surface and slice evenly against the grain of the meat. Repeat with second half breast when additional slices are needed.

237

STORING LEFTOVERS

Handling cooked turkey incorrectly can result in food poisoning. Think of the post-cooking stage as a countdown that begins when you take the turkey out of the oven. From that time, you have approximately 2 hours to serve it and then refrigerate or freeze the leftovers—the turkey, stuffing, and gravy. Why just two hours? Because bacteria that cause food poisoning can multiply to undesirable levels on perishable food left at room temperature for longer than that.

It is important to take out all of the stuffing from the turkey as soon as you remove the bird from the oven. Extra stuffing can be kept hot in the oven at 200°F while you eat, or can be refrigerated.

How you store the leftovers is also important in preventing bacterial growth. Large quantities should be divided into smaller portions and stored in several small or shallow covered containers. That's because food in small amounts will get cold more quickly.

Leftover turkey will keep in the refrigerator for 3 to 4 days. Stuffing and gravy should be used within 1 to 2 days. Bring leftover gravy to a rolling boil before serving.

For longer storage, package items in freezer paper or heavy-duty aluminum foil and freeze them. Proper wrapping will prevent "freezer burn"—white dried-out patches on the surface of food that make it tough and tasteless. Don't forget to date your packages and use the oldest ones first. Frozen turkey, stuffing, and gravy should be used within 1 month.

QUOTES ON HUNTING

*Solitary hunting suits anyone
who needs religion in his life but not congregations.
The vaulting sky over a marsh is higher than the tallest
cathedral. The marsh is grander than the greatest temple.
The day dawns just for you and the ducks. It is a soul-
wrenching experience—a lesson of mortality amid an
infinitude of life. Solitary visits to a marsh transfigure mere
duck hunters into the most profound impediment of the
sporting fraternity, the wildfowler.*

George Reiger,
The Wildfowler's Quest, *1989*

*The real hunter is probably as free
as it's possible for modern man to be in this teeming
technocracy of ours. Not because he sheds civilized codes
and restraints when he goes into the woods, becoming an
animal, but because he can project himself out of and
beyond himself and be wholly absorbed in a quieter,
deeper and older world.*

John Madson, 1979,
John Madson: Out Home

239

Hunting is one of the last genuine,
personal adventures of modern man. Just as game animals
are the truest indicators of quality natural environment, so
hunting is the truest indicator of quality natural freedom.

John Madson, 1979,
John Madson: Out Home

The unskilled shooter, by crippling,
often kills more birds than the good shot without knowing
it. This is not something to laugh off, like poor card sense or
a tin ear for music. If you are going to shoot, you have a
sporting responsibility to shoot well—not to kill more but to
kill more cleanly.

George Bird Evans,
The Upland Shooting Life, *1971*

The aloneness of the hunter,
and his thoughts of his hunting past, are the very genesis of
primitive energy. He is always a young man, then, and
making his most daring journeys. He will not think of
middle age, and even the responsibility of his family will be
dim as he pauses, every sense alert for the sound of what he
plans to kill. This reality is the only time that he is fully
alive. All the rest is the dreaming time.

Franklin Russell,
The Hunting Animal, *1983*

*It would be less than honest
to maintain that all hunters are upright gentlemen,
or even true sportsmen. But I'll bet that if all boys were
taught the joys of hunting and appreciation of the out-of-
doors, half our psychiatrists, social workers, policemen
and prison guards would be out of work when the next
generation takes over.*

Ned Smith,
Gone for the Day, *1971*

*When you hunt and fish you collect
times, places and minor events that last a lifetime
and the fellow beside you collects his own, which may be
completely different.*

Charles F. Waterman,
Times and Places, Home and Away, *1988*

*For millions of years we survived as hunters.
In the few short millennia since our divorce from that
necessity there has been no time for significant biological
change—anatomical, physiological, or behavioral. Today,
we have small hope of comprehending ourselves and our
world unless we understand that man still, in his innermost
being, remains a hunter.*

Robert Ardrey, The Hunting Hypothesis,
an epilogue in Douglas McDougall's book,
8 Bore Ammunition, *1985*

*In a hunting trip the days of long monotony
in getting to the ground, and the days of unrequited toil
after it has been reached, always far outnumber the red-
letter days of success. But it is just these times of failure that
really test the hunter. In the long run, common sense and
dogged perseverance avail him more than any other
qualities. The man who does not give up, but hunts steadily
and resolutely through the spells of bad luck until the luck
turns, is the man who wins success in the end.*

Theodore Roosevelt,
The Wilderness Hunter, *1893*

*What friends I have, what days I treasure most,
what places that I think about and smile…they are because
shotguns are. Without them I would have been empty. They
have made my life full.*

Gene Hill,
Hill Country—Our World Without Shotguns, *1981*

*I do not hunt for the joy of killing
but for the joy of living, and for the inexpressible pleasure of
mingling my life, however briefly, with that of a wild
creature that I respect, admire, and value.*

John Madson,
John Madson, Out Home, *1979*

*I've never known an outdoorsman
who owned all the gear he thought he needed. Even if he
owns it, the odds are that he can't find it.*

Charley Dickey,
Movin' Along with Charley Dickey, *1985*

INDEX

245

246

248

THE NATIONAL WILD TURKEY FEDERATION

HISTORY, PURPOSE, AND PROGRAMS

History: The NWTF was incorporated as a private, nonprofit conservation and education organization in Fredericksburg, VA, in 1973. The Federation moved its headquarters to Edgefield, SC, that same year. It remains there today, housed in the Wild Turkey Center.

The Federation is a grassroots, volunteer organization, governed by a 19-member board of directors. NWTF volunteers are organized in a state and local chapter system. South Carolina was chartered as the first NWTF state chapter in 1974; the Georgia and Kentucky chapters received charters later that year. There are currently 48 state and 740 local chapters in the NWTF chapter system. There were about 1,300 Federation members by the end of 1973, compared to 120,000 members in December 1995.

Recent awards to the Federation include the Outdoor Writers Association of America Mountain of Jade Award (1987) "for distinguished effort to improve the quality of America's great outdoors and thus add to the enjoyment of all outdoor people"; The Wildlife Society's Group Achievement Award (1988), the Chevron Conservation Award (1990) "for exceptional service in the cause of conservation"; and The Southeast Section of the Wildlife Society's Outstanding Book Award (1993).

Purpose: The mission statement of the National Wild Turkey Federation clearly defines its purpose: the conservation of the wild turkey and the preservation of the turkey hunting tradition. Focusing on the wild turkey but benefitting a variety of natural resources, the NWTF accomplishes its mission by working on many fronts, forging relationships and uniting diverse groups toward common goals.

Programs: NWTF programs are many and varied, such as the Banquet Program and Project HELP, which offers people seeds to help grow habitat that in turn helps the turkey. These programs, and many others, are funded through the Wild Turkey Super Fund, an account that pools monies generated by NWTF chapters and individual, government, and corporate contributors into State and National Super Funds jointly administered by the NWTF, its state chapters, and their respective wildlife agencies.

HOW TO BECOME A MEMBER

If you are one of those people who believes in putting more back into America's wildlife than you take, then this National Wild Turkey Federation offer is for you. For a limited time only the NWTF will send you, absolutely FREE, a camo cap plus our new "Turkey Hunting With The Legends" video, 6 issues of award-winning *Turkey Call* magazine, and 4 issues of *The Caller* when you join The National Wild Turkey Federation today.

That's right, FREE! Send in your $25 membership today and receive our special NWTF cap and video, NWTF decal, 6 issues of America's Number One turkey hunter's magazine, and 4 issues of *The Caller*. At the same time, you'll be supporting the vital research and management efforts of the nonprofit National Wild Turkey Federation.

YES! I'd like to join the NWTF, a nonprofit corporation dedicated to the conservation of the American wild turkey. Start my subscription to Turkey Call, and send my Free camo cap, video, decal, and membership card. Sign me up as a:

☐ Full Voting Member - $25   ☐ Sponsor Member - $200
☐ PAYMENT ENCLOSED   ☐ Incentive Camo Cap

PLEASE PRINT

Charge my   MasterCard   Visa # _____ Exp. Date _____

Signature (if charge) _____

Name _____ Social Security # _____

Address _____

City _____ State _____ Zip _____

To order return to: The National Wild Turkey Federation, Post Office Box 530, Edgefield, South Carolina 29824, Phone 803-637-3106 or Call 1-800-THE NWTF.

Annual membership in the NWTF is $25 of which $5 is for a subscription to *Turkey Call*, and $1 for *The Caller*. Single copy price for either publication is $3.50. Dues in excess of $6, and all contributions, are deemed to have been made to a qualifying 501(c)(3) organization and may be deductible on your tax returns.

NATIONAL WILD TURKEY FEDERATION

JAKES

AMERICA'S YOUTH —WORKING FOR THE WILD TURKEY
— 17 years old and under —

The return of the wild turkey across America has enabled sportsmen in forty-nine (49) states to marvel at the beauty and splendor of this great game bird. This heritage must be passed on to future generations to enjoy. Help us by enlisting your son or daughter in the NWTF youth program, JAKES (Juniors Acquiring Knowledge, Ethics, and Sportsmanship.)

Membership in the JAKES program helps to ensure that your son or daughter will enjoy a lifetime commitment to wildlife conservation. Sign them up now. We must involve the youth of America in this important conservation effort.

JAKES MISSION STATEMENT

The National Wild Turkey Federation's JAKES (Juniors Acquiring Knowledge, Ethics and Sportsmanship) program is dedicated to informing, educating and involving America's youth in wildlife conservation and the wise stewardship of our natural resources.

YES! Please enroll this young person as a JAKES member and send a membership card, decal, patch, and four (4) issues of *The Caller* newsletter.

PLEASE PRINT

Name _____

Address _____

City _____ State _____ Zip _____

Sponsored by: _____

Address, if different from above _____

_____

Mail check for $5 to:
The National Wild Turkey Federation,
Post Office Box 530, Edgefield, SC 29824

WILD ABOUT TURKEY

The National Wild Turkey Federation
P.O. Box 530
Edgefield, SC 29824
1-800-THE-NWTF

Please send _____ copies of *Wild About Turkey*

@ $19.95 each_____

South Carolina residents add sales tax @ $ 1.20 each_____

Postage and handling @ $5.00 each_____

Total_____

Charge to Visa (   ) or MasterCard (   )

_____ Expiration Date_____

Signature _____

Name_____

Address _____

City _____ State _____ Zip _____

COOKBOOK LOVERS
TAKE NOTE...

If you've enjoyed *Wild About Turkey*, The Wimmer Companies, Inc., has a catalog of 250 other cookbook titles that may interest you. To receive your free copy, write:

The Wimmer Companies, Inc.
4210 B. F. Goodrich Boulevard
Memphis, Tennessee 38118
or
call 1-800-727-1034